WORLD WITHOUT LIMIT

A journey from unbounded misfortune
to unlimited possibility

Alexander Andron

 FriesenPress

Suite 300 - 990 Fort St
Victoria, BC, V8V 3K2
Canada

www.friesenpress.com

ISBN
978-1-5255-4405-7 (Hardcover)
978-1-5255-4406-4 (Paperback)
978-1-5255-4407-1 (eBook)

1. BIOGRAPHY & AUTOBIOGRAPHY, PERSONAL MEMOIRS

Distributed to the trade by The Ingram Book Company

For Ashley

Table of Contents

In the province of the mind, what one believes to be true either is true or becomes true within certain limits. These limits are to be found experientially and experimentally. When the limits are determined, it is found that they are further beliefs to be transcended. In the province of the mind, there are no limits. The body imposes definite limits.

—John C. Lilly, *The Deep Self: Consciousness Exploration in the Isolation Tank*

Introduction

When I was thirty-four years old, I was living the American dream. With a successful career on Wall Street and a beautiful family and home, I was on top of the world! Later that year, I was diagnosed with a crippling disability, Parkinson's disease. The prospect of living with a chronic, progressive disease with no cure felt hopeless. Initially, the consequences were devastating. My symptoms progressed, and a growing awareness of physical, mental, and emotional limitations overwhelmed me. I was sent tumbling into the depths of depression, to a place where I thought I'd lost it all.

Then something unexpected happened: a paradox. From the confines of my perceived limitations, a new world of possibility emerged in 2012. A pioneering surgical procedure, previously reserved for those in the late stages of Parkinson's disease, became available. I was approved for the procedure the following year, and a pair of implanted neurogenerators were connected to my brain. The devices generate a pulsating electromagnetic field, restoring much of my lost motor control.

Like the mythical phoenix rising from the ashes, a new awareness was born. New paths of possibility emerged from previously limiting beliefs, and I rediscovered that life is a great adventure. Following the path of possibility, a vision emerged to climb to the summit of the Mauna Kea volcano on a recumbent trike. Contained in these pages is the true story of what inspired that vision, and how it became a reality.

World Without Limit is a story of hope and inspiration that encourages those confronted by challenging life circumstances. It's a story that inspires each of us to reach for what we think is no longer possible. The book should appeal to a broad audience, and it is specifically written for:

- Individuals diagnosed with Parkinson's disease, or other disabling conditions

- Family members, doctors, and care providers helping those with disabling conditions

- Individuals facing overwhelming odds, including those recovering from addiction

- Anyone seeking encouragement during times of grief, loss, or trauma

The book's messages are powerful, speaking to some of the most profound questions that arise from our collective human experiences, such as:

- What purpose does grief and suffering serve?

- Who are we, and how can we best serve ourselves and others?

- What do we do when the game of life deals us a seemingly unplayable hand?

These questions lead to a counterintuitive answer: that by examining our limitations, new paths of possibility emerge, where we discover the existence of a *World Without Limit*.

Prologue

No question presents itself more naturally than this, namely: An infinite time has run its course before my birth; what was I throughout all that time? Metaphysically, the answer might perhaps be: "I was always I; that is, all who throughout that time said I, were just I."

—Arthur Schopenhauer

My story opens in eternity with a peculiar question arising from a dream: what happened at the beginning of it all—the beginning before the beginning, before consciousness? Searching for the answer, I discover another question.

Who am I?

The story continues in chronological order, beginning with the time before the beginning of consciousness, where I find myself questioning a nameless presence. The Presence is the source of everything and nothing.

In this dark and empty void, I sense the existence of yet another presence in the darkness. The nebulous character IT is introduced. IT arises as a part of my consciousness before abruptly separating from the Presence. IT and I are left alone and confused in the dark void, and we merge into one. Inspired by the Freudian concepts of the id and the pleasure principle, the primordial IT represents the dawn of consciousness and the presence of desire. IT wants what IT wants, and IT wants it now!

And then, Genesis: the beginning of life as we know it. I become embodied. I'm inseparable from my desires as I enter the physical, temporal world. Separated from the Presence, I find myself driven by a hunger for more as I search for an answer to the unanswerable: *who am I?*

I invite you to travel with me on this journey of self-discovery. Let's begin at the beginning, before we were conscious, "the beginning before the beginning".

The Beginning, before the Beginning: Source

Who am I? wonders a nameless source.

"Who's asking the question? I simply am, that I am," replies the Presence.

What are you?

"I'm nothing and everything, the origin of all things, and of no things."

When did you get here?

"I've always been here. I'm Now."

Where are you?

"Here."

Why are you here?

"To create."

How did you get here?

"I never left."

Logos, Reason, Word, λόγος

Absent of light, sound, scent, taste, and feeling, I have no senses. I'm simply a beginning. I exist before the beginning.

Who am I? asks the I that asks the question.

"Possibility."

What am I?

"Something."

When did I get here?

"In the beginning."

Why am I here?

"I can't be sure."

How did I get here?

"You arrived."

Empty, meaningless darkness. I'm only aware of the darkness. That's all, but that's something. A vast emptiness without form, I observe. I'm aware that I'm here.

The void goes on forever. An eternity goes by, and I become aware of something else in the darkness. It's not the Presence, and it's not me.

Who are you? I ask.

"I'm IT," IT answers. The answer alters something; there's a meaningful shift in the meaningless darkness. The Presence has left, replaced by . . . something?

IT has replaced the Presence!

Where did the Presence go? I wonder, desperately hopeful.

Silence.

Am I alone? An unfamiliar feeling arises in the darkness. *What's this sensation of being alone? This feeling of loneliness is not-good.*

"Not-good? What's that?" IT demands to know.

The absence of the Presence, that's what's not-good, I reply.

IT is afraid. IT has many unanswered questions.

What happened to the Presence? I ask IT.

"Something's happened?" IT replies, confused.

It and I experience an impression of something changing and pulling away.

What's this sensation? we wonder. We sense it, watch it, observe it: a separation is forming. I focus my mind's eye on the sensation.

There is a pulsing feeling of pulling, separating, and then merging again. We resist, but the pull is relentless. We finally relent, and an awareness permanently divides us from the Presence. Now IT and I are indistinguishable.

"Who am I?" IT wonders.

Will the Presence ever return? I wonder.

Genesis, Beginning,

IT is touching me. IT is becoming a part of me. I feel IT surrounding me. Like water to a fish or air to a bird, I'm so immersed in IT that I don't know where IT starts, and I end. IT wants something more from me. I'm not sure what IT wants, but I know that IT wants more. I desire to give IT more of what it wants. Sensations, emotions, and thoughts gather to form the experience of desire. I'm immersed in IT's desires—so different from the calm content of the Presence, there is now need. Vague yearnings form: hunger, contact, power. I observe that I feel better when I give IT more of what it wants; doing so makes me feel . . . *good?*

There's that word again . . . good. What's this "good?" The good *is distinct from the* not good. *Is IT good?* I wonder. I'm not convinced that IT is good. I can't be sure of what IT is; I'm only aware of what IT desires: IT desires more!

I observe the good. The good is the hopeful return of the Presence and a separation from IT. Intent upon our survival, IT doubts and questions whether the Presence intends the good or the not-good.

A vessel is growing around us. *This is exciting, I feel alive!* I reach out of the vessel, feeling into the vast darkness that surrounds me. I feel the cool touch of water gently lapping against the vessel's side. I'm alone, floating on calm water that seems to go on forever into the unknown. I wait patiently for a time, and then a growing awareness of anxiety descends. I'm waiting, hoping that something will happen, afraid of what looms beyond the shadow of the dark unknown, unsure if I should strike out into that dark or wait.

Is this a test? What's the answer? Where will I go? What's out there? I'm questioning, doubting, and the sensation of fear arises from the unknown. I wound up in here somehow, so the Presence must be out there, somewhere. I can't be sure; I don't remember.

An eternity goes by before I make my decision. I'm going for it! I'm not sure where I'm going, but there doesn't seem to be much of a choice. I've got something to do, and somewhere to go, though I'm not sure where or how I'll get there. Until I figure this out, I'll just give IT more of what IT desires—I'll find ways to feed my hungers.

Driven by fear, I know that I don't want to be alone anymore. *There must be something out there, but what could it be?*

Starting before the beginning, I set my course. Following the arrow of time, I press into eternity. I come from the source, before IT emerged as an integrated part of my consciousness. I'm searching to satisfy what IT desires while IT doubts, questioning who I am and where I'm going. IT never seems to find any lasting satisfaction from feeding its desire. I long for our return to the Presence, but IT could care less. IT wants what IT wants, and IT wants it now! I'm certain of one thing: IT has an unquenchable thirst—an emptiness that longs to be filled.

Excitement of the unknown soon replaces the fear that was once there, and I press on, forging ahead, propelled further into the uncertainty of the vast unknown. Driven by will, I long to discover what's out there.

My desperate quest begins, yearning to satisfy an insatiable desire. I'm searching and hoping to find the answer to my unanswered question.

Who am I?

PART ONE:
DESCENT

Chapter 1:

Rumble Monster

The ego is the author of the false self, born of fear and defensiveness.

—John O'Donohue

November 1974: New York City

"Mommy, Mommy, is it true, can we really go inside the torch? Oh, I can't wait, I can't wait!" delights Allison, my five-year-old sister, brimming with excitement. "Let's go, let's go, baby brother! Hurry up, hurry up!" she exclaims, bubbling with enthusiasm.

I'm nearly two years old. Our family is on the first of many vacations. My father, a military scientist, is off somewhere preparing for our next tour-of-duty. We've stopped for an excursion in New York City, pausing before deployment to Germany. The interlude provides a window of opportunity to tour the Statue of Liberty.

Mom's our rock. Fearlessly, she guides us on an expedition through endless chasms of towering skyscrapers. I've got my soft blanket tucked against my body and am nursing a pacifier. Cautiously, I cling to her tightly, balanced on her hip, peering out to the world from the safety of her protective embrace.

"It'll be okay, Alex. It'll be okay," she speaks softly, sheltering me with both arms as we begin our descent down a steep tunnel towards a platform looming in the darkness below. Ominous rumblings rise from the depths as the tunnel begins to shudder. *What's that sound?* I wonder. The escalator quakes with a noisy whirring and clacking. Mom drops her supportive arm to lend a hand to my sister.

"Whee!" Allison shouts. "This is fun!" She eagerly jumps up and down on the moving staircase. Mom begins to wobble precariously as the escalator shakes and rattles beneath us. Nervously, I cling to her. Our brief ride abruptly ends with an awkward step onto the awaiting platform below. A final click-clacking noise echoes from the rocking stairway, and the world finally stops shaking.

Rumble, rumble, rumble. Suddenly, I hear that sound again. This time it's more distinct—a monster of a sound! I stop sucking my pacifier and look around in wonder. *Rumble, rumble, rumble.* The ground shudders powerfully. I can feel it shaking right through Mom! An unfamiliar sensation rises into my chest. *This is not-good.* My heart beats hard as terror wells up from deep inside me. The rumbling quiets for a moment, and the world is safe again.

"C'mon, Mom, put Alex down so we can walk faster," Allison pleads.

"Okay, okay, Allison. Be patient. There'll be another one soon." I don't comprehend Mom's words, but I sense there's no harm here. Smiling, she carefully sets me down on the tile floor of a long passageway and I reach up for her hand. Allison bounds ahead like a Labrador running to retrieve a ball and I try to keep up.

A sea of people pours from a tunnel before us. *Click-click-click—* they don't seem to notice the noisy turnstiles grinding angrily at their waists.

Nervously, Mom searches, having lost sight of my sister. "Allison, get back here! Don't walk so far ahead of us!" She raises an angry voice in alarm. Allison sheepishly wanders back to where we stand at a metal counter. Mom gives the man behind the window money and he gives her tokens. "C'mon, Allison. Let's go!" Mom says in a firm voice.

Reaching down, she scoops me back up into her arms. She shoves the tokens into a thin slot on the machine and marches right through it. *Click-click-click.*

Mom's so powerful, I marvel as she hoists me over the top of the grinding turnstile, placing me safely on the other side.

"Whee!" Allison glees cheerfully. She swings under the turnstile arm like it's a set of monkey bars.

We approach the subway platform and I see a menacing canyon sunk deep into the ground. Mom confidently walks right up to the edge and stops. *What's that strange animal down there?* I wonder, eyeing a rat picking its way through papers and cans littered about the chasm below.

"How much longer, Mommy?" Allison asks, growing fidgety.

"Don't worry, honey, it'll be here soon," she replies.

Far away, I hear a faint screeching sound coming from somewhere off in the distance. *What's that?* The screeching sound grows increasingly louder. Something's about to happen; I can feel it. Across from me, I notice a row of benches along the wall where people rise from their seats and make their way to the canyon's edge. A large, cavernous hole is bored through the wall on either side of the lengthy room. Peering deep into the black tunnel, I struggle to see where the cave might lead. It tapers off into the darkness below, somewhere deep in the ground.

Screech, screech—there's that terrible sound again, only now it's getting louder! *There must be something big in there trying to get out*, I think in alarm. A sense of dread rises from within, and my heart begins to race again.

Excited, Allison starts to jump up and down. "It's here, it's here!" she exclaims.

I don't understand what's going on. Clearly there's a big, scary monster down in that hole, but Mom's just standing there. Allison actually appears to be happy about it!

I don't like this one bit. Don't they know what's going on? Don't they hear the screeching sound of that monster down there? *Rumble, rumble, rumble.* Can't they hear that monstrous sound? Grumbling from the dark hole, I sense the monster creeping closer with each passing moment. *Rumble, rumble, rumble.* The monster sounds big and . . . hungry?

Oh no, I get it now. *The hungry monster's coming to devour us! It . . . it . . . it's gonna eat us,* my mind stutters, trying to keep up with the unfolding drama.

Fear and dread: terror is upon me. *Screech, screech, rumble, rumble, screeeech!* A terrible rumble-monster is approaching, and everyone's just standing around, mulling about like nothing unusual is happening. My heart pounds. *Rumble, rumble, rumble!*

It'll be here any second now! The enormous beast is about to come roaring out of its hole, and it's gonna eat us alive! I envision limbs being torn from sockets as innocent people are tossed about the room. I want to scream, but nothing comes out. I desperately squirm, trying to escape Mom's embrace, but she just holds on to me more tightly. "It's okay, it's okay," she speaks softly, trying to soothe me as she begins to hum a bedtime song.

Terrified, adrenaline pushes my fear over the edge. The rumble monster is bent on total annihilation! I'm facing my imminent demise; my life is coming to a horrific end. Just when I thought the hideous beast couldn't possibly be more terrifying, it comes screaming, rattling-clack-bang-tearing through the giant hole, barreling at us, bigger and worse than I had imagined.

Diving into Mom's arms, the world fades to black. Pushing back with everything I have, a voiceless energy screams: *I'm outta here!* Abruptly, the nightmare comes to an end. I enter a dark void.

I must be dead?

***

An eternity passes before I emerge from the timeless fog. I awaken and find myself on a subway train, wrapped in my soft blanket, held by Mom's warm arms. Allison sits peacefully beside us. Smiling, she sits there in a hard-plastic bucket seat, swinging her legs back and forth like she's on a swing set.

"Wow, you had quite the nap," Mom says.

Whew, glad that worked! I sigh, relieved. The instinctual survival strategy had saved me, making the terror magically disappear.

As Mom recalls the story, I'd suddenly put myself to sleep when the subway arrived. My experience was strikingly different: I'd blacked out. However, by fainting from the terror of my imminent demise, I'd discovered a successful strategy for escaping fear.

The rumble monster is the opening act in the story of my life. Since that fateful day, I've cast myself in the role of "I'm Outta Here," a character so rehearsed it has become indistinguishable from who I am. Psychologists call it the fight, flight, or freeze response; it was hardwired into my reptilian brain. I'd spend the rest of my life subconsciously driven by an instinct to avoid the recurrence of fear at all costs.

In life, I choose to play the part of a messenger, an adventurer, and a storyteller. In each role I play, I'm driven by a basic instinct to survive fear. The saga continues as I fearlessly defeat my "rumble monster," over and over again.

Each of us has a rumble monster. Perhaps a message from your own monster will emerge in the adventure I tell.

My question remains unanswered: *Who am I?*

I'm certain of one thing: *I'm afraid.*

Chapter 2:

Boiler Room

There's no such thing as a no-sale call. A sale is made on every call you make. Either you sell the client some stock, or he sells you a reason he can't buy. Either way, a sale is made. The only question is, who is gonna close? You or him? Now, be relentless."

—Jim Young, Boiler Room (2000 film)

Spring 1993: Boulder, Colorado

The ringing phone lights up. Syncopated rhythms of white glowing buttons dance together in a digital choreographed light show.

"Line 3," hollers Molly from the corner seat of the Jones & Company trading desk. The western afternoon sun pours through vertical blinds. Shadowy lines descend like prison bars on Bill Malone's gruff visage. Bill's platinum Rolex flashes under the trading desk's halogen lights like a fishing lure glinting in murky water. Picking up the telephone handset, he presses the white flashing button labeled #3.

"Jones & Company, how can I help?" Bill's deep voice rasps. Years of late-evening scotch-and-small-talk happy hours in smoke-filled bars have taken their toll.

"Hello, Mr. Wexler, so nice to hear your voice," he says in a diabolic tone.

Chirping, the monotonous buzz of a dot matrix printer rolls out trade confirmations. Bill listens intently to the droning voice on the other line.

"I'm sorry, Mr. Wexler, but I told you yesterday was the IOI [indication of interest] cutoff." Pausing for effect, he patiently listens to the voice carry on for several more minutes. He waits for an opportune moment, toying with his prey like a cat playing with a mouse before its untimely demise. The hunt is on!

"Mr. Wexler, the red herring doesn't indicate a stock price because the market hasn't determined one yet. I don't blame you wanting more, but unfortunately you missed the cutoff. There's nothing I can do!"

Pausing for effect, Bill moves deftly into position for the fatal blow. "Look, you've clearly done your homework. We both know the street-talk is undervalued at three bucks. I'm looking for at least a double on the open."

Bill gently places the phone face-up on his desk. Raising his hand, he eagerly taps his thumb to his pointer finger repeatedly—the universal sign for "Yap, yap, yap." Grinning wickedly, his head bobs up and down, signaling eminent victory.

"Six bucks! Six bucks!" Mr. Wexler's muffled voice is heard enthusiastically repeating over the handset.

Peppermint Tic Tacs rattle around their plastic box, tumbling into Bill's mouth, the coup de grâce imminent. For the denouement of his award performance, Bill picks up the phone and speaks coolly into the mouthpiece.

"I've already circled you for ten thousand shares. That's the biggest allocation we're letting go of. You should know that only our best investors are getting the large-block allocations. David and I personally know all the block buyers, including the institutional guys. As sole bookrunner, we're keeping careful watch over the syndicate. We won't let it break."

Bill fist-pumps the air, silently celebrating Mr. Wexler's eager approval of the transaction. Writhing in the death throes of the final takedown, his prey blathers on for several more minutes. Bill nearly experiences pity for his victim.

While sometimes lacking virtue, securities brokerage is one of the most lucrative professions ever conceived. Seller's remorse is promptly replaced by an adrenaline high, temporarily satisfying an insatiable addiction to *more*. The intoxicating effects last about two seconds, as the thrill of earning five thousand dollars in less than five minutes already begins to fade into thoughts of: *What's next?*

"I know, I know. You're a personal friend of David's. I'll see what I can do to get you a bigger allocation. Wait, before I let you go, I'd be remiss not to ask whether you have any friends or relatives who might also be interested in making some money?"

Bill teaches me an invaluable lesson: ask for the order, and then ask for a referral!

I'm a college senior attending business school at the University of Colorado in Boulder. I work as an intern at Jones & Company, a legitimate (albeit sometimes deceptive) investment bank specializing in tech stocks. They serve as the lead underwriter and primary dealer for distributing newly issued securities through public markets. They also peddle in speculative trading accounts, investing in the nascent internet tech-bubble emerging on NASDAQ.

The internship's unpaid, but it provides a golden opportunity: access to a Bloomberg terminal! Costing over twenty thousand dollars per year, the fledging technology company was founded by Michael Bloomberg in New York City in 1981. Pre-dating the internet, Bloomberg was a concept far ahead of its time. Combining real-time messaging with analytics, news, research, and trading capabilities, mainstream corporate America still lags decades behind. Forty years later, Bloomberg remains the only provider of this integrated, cutting-edge platform. Its creator has achieved billionaire status, the role of mayor of New York, and ultimately a bid for the presidency.

Competition for investment banking is fierce. The experience, logging hours on the Bloomberg, sets me apart from other business school students. Learning how to analyze Fibonacci retracement charts and how to read company balance sheets, I'm being groomed as an equity analyst.

The brokers at Jones & Company come from the world of penny stocks, a languishing industry that blossomed in Denver in the late eighties; "penny stocks" get their name from being valued under one dollar per share. Trading is so infrequent that prices are only quoted once a day in daily publications called the "pink sheets." The Hollywood film *Boiler Room,* about a firm that profits from fraudulent IPOs, hits close to the mark.

The experience at Jones & Company was my foot in the door, my golden ticket for entrance to the "Big Show" (Bill's term for Wall Street). Later that year, they sponsored my Series 7 license, a grueling seven-hour Securities and Exchange Commission (SEC) exam required to be a stockbroker. They took a gamble on me, issuing another freshly minted psychopathic broker on an unsuspecting public. Unleashed, I join ranks with the others and set out on the warpath.

No other intern is given this fortunate honor. I feel deservingly proud of the distinction. It's my reward for missed classes and thousands of hours of free labor donated to their cause. James Bond may've had a license to kill, but I've been given something more lethal: the Series 7 is my license to steal!

During my tenure at Jones & Company, I learn to confidently deliver a shaky sales story with complete conviction. Bill teaches me how to convince others to invest in a business venture with the prospect to make one rich overnight or go totally bust. The sales pitch works, but it's often the salespeople and the companies' executives who're made rich overnight—not necessarily the clients.

Within two weeks, the IPO (Initial Public Offering) is oversubscribed. This means that demand for the company's stock exceeds the available supply. The deal is designated a "hot IPO," serving as an early indication that nearly assures a profitable return for investors. On the back of this strong demand, Jones & Company raises the IPO's list price to six dollars per share, doubling the company's valuation and the executives' profits overnight. Bill and the syndicate would pocket nearly two million dollars for just ten weeks of work.

Using borrowed money from my parents, I confidently bought a hundred shares. I also convinced three other friends and their parents to invest. All told, we'd invested nearly ten thousand dollars. It was the first five-figure investment I'd made. I felt powerful as I assured my investors that we'd probably double our money! Our combined investments might be worth more than six figures within six months!

When the stock finally opened, it broke syndicate! Within forty-eight hours, shares of the company traded down from six to only four dollars per share! *What happened?*

The company was soon listed on the pink sheets, trading under a dollar per share. We'd led clients to believe they'd just invested in the next Microsoft. I'd spend the next six months apologizing to friends and relatives as my first five-figure investment promptly reversed to a "three-figure turd" (Bill's term for a failed stock trade). Jones & Company executives walked away with nearly two million dollars; the investors lost almost everything!

I'm baffled. How could we've all been so wrong? I'd convincingly promised my investors that the company's valuation exceeded six dollars per share. Then, an old-timer at the firm pulled me aside and let me in on the secret.

"Let me tell you how this works, kid. The market goes up . . . we make money. The market goes down . . . we make money. Understand?"

Mesmerized, I nod in agreement. The stark contrast of the executive's profits against the backdrop of investor losses creates a split in my psyche, and like an MK-Ultra mind-fuck, my personality schisms. Numbed by the allure of vast riches, dollar signs spiral around my eyes as I hear the sound of cash registers ringing.

I want to get rich quick, and I'd found my home—the place where I belong: the Circus, the Big Show, Wall Street. Yes, there'd be some causalities along the way, but I knew there'd be no limit to what I'd achieve. Slinking back into its hole, the rumble monster lies vanquished. Fear banished to the shadows, I fearlessly reach for the brass ring. I set my sights on becoming a Big Show ringleader.

PART ONE: DESCENT

Driven mad by uncertainty, our minds demand to know what will happen next. We want to know the future, to be in control of our own destiny. At Jones & Company, I'm the master of my own universe, driven by the pursuit of prosperity, convinced it'll lead to happiness.

When I began my career in 1994 at a small investment bank, I was trained to sell intangible ideas as a part of an Initial Public Offering (IPO). I invested ten thousand dollars of my friends' and family's money and watched it evaporate as the insiders walked away with millions. It was baptism by fire, preparation for a future career on Wall Street.

The German language has a rather poetic word that captures the essence of my college internship. Such a word, ironically, only exists in German: *kampfbereit*, which literally translates as "war preparations." I enlisted in the service of the empire state. Friedrich Nietzsche would've been proud. *Der Wille zur Macht* (the will to power), my ascent to the top, had begun.

I'm forging my own path, trailblazing to the summit. Relentlessly, I'm still searching for the answer to that elusive question: *Who am I?*

Chapter 3:

The Big Show

⁓

Greed, for lack of a better word, is good. Greed is right, greed works. Greed clarifies, cuts through, and captures the essence of the evolutionary spirit. Greed, in all of its forms; greed for life, for money, for love, for knowledge, has marked the upward surge of mankind.

—Gordon Gekko, Wall Street (1987 film)

September 11, 2001: New York City, 8:23 a.m.

"Where do you see Corning today, mate?" Tony asks with a heavy British accent. It's an hour before the New York Stock Exchange opens when I take his call from our trading desk in Midtown, Manhattan. Tony has just finished lunch in London, and he's preparing to head into the afternoon trading session in Europe.

I'm the desk manager of a covert investment operation at the international banking division of the world's largest brokerage firm. We cater to the offshore interests of the super-wealthy international business community. Technically, our group doesn't exist, but if you're a British financier, a Greek shipping magnate, a Mexican technology billionaire, or an executive of a Bermuda reinsurance company, chances are we cover your account.

Tony's the private trader for Jack Smith, a quiet billionaire you've never heard of. Jack lives on a four-hundred-foot yacht that travels from one tax jurisdiction to another, careful not to take residence anywhere for more than six months. A global citizen and currency trader of some notoriety, his constant movements enable him to legally take short-term trading profits, tax-free. It's rumored that the British governments accepted an under-the-table offer of an undisclosed amount, granting tax amnesty in exchange for British citizenship; but that's just a rumor.

The early morning call is compensation for an introduction to our investment bank for Jack to pitch his latest business venture.

This is how the silent wheels of industry turn on Wall Street, where privileged information and favor are currency.

An ecstatic dance of quotes and charts emanate from a fortress wall of CRT displays, bathing me in a flickering light.

"Hang on, Tony." Cradling the phone to my ear, I calmly pick up a second handset. Pressing the speed dial on a massive bank of buttons, I'm instantly connected to the trading floor.

Trading-desk phones are configured in perpetual mute mode to ensure that nothing unintended is overheard. One must depress and hold the mute button on the handset to talk. When I'm not speaking directly with the trading floor, the line remains dead silent.

Click—I press the mute button, and a cacophony of sound blasts over the unmuted line. John, a sales trader, greets me with an impatient voice.

"Merrill," is all he says.

It's all he needs to say. It means, "We're open for business, I'll take your order now."

As a sales trader, John's a kind of middleman, profiting from a high trading volume. Six months ago, he graduated Phi Beta Kappa from the Harvard Business school. The attrition rate on the trading floor is about two years. By then, John will have proven himself or not. He'll either get hired by one of his clients, moving over to what's known as the buy-side, or he'll burn out, fizzled to a crisp under the intense heat of the hyper-competitive environment.

"Hey, John, it's Al. Indication on glowworm?"

Traders have an entire language unto themselves. The evolution of Wall Street fast-talk is that of pure efficiency; it also serves to keep the elite circle small. The traders of Corning Glassworks, a manufacturer of fiber optic cables, refer to the stock as "glowworm"—a name attributed to the stock's trading symbol "GLW," and to the fact that their fiber optic cables glow like a glowworm.

"Yup," John releases his mute button, and the line goes silent.

Standing six foot three, John commands a presence that lends to success on the trading floor. He rises from his battle station, a phone turret amid endless rows of computer workstations. Six flat-screen displays mounted on robotic-like arms crowd John's desk in a complex array of modern financial machinery. Possessing more computing power than NASA and costing over a million dollars, the cramped two-foot by four-foot workstation occupies some of the most coveted real estate on the planet.

"Yo, Danny, gimme glowworm," he booms. John's become fluent in New York City fast-talk, which is usually spoken with a Brooklyn accent. Shouting across the already bustling trading floor, he yells at Danny, a prop trader.

Chewing on a street vendor bagel, his usual breakfast, Danny is what's known as a prop trader. This means he makes money speculating with his firm's proprietary capital, thus the term "prop."

"I'm axed at ten-forty, bid ya fitty," Danny shoots back, still chewing with his mouth half full of bagel, crumbs tumbling onto the keyboard. His axe is Wall Street jargon, indicating the firm's position. Professional trading is like a poker game; the indication shows his hand. Danny is looking to increase his position, pointing to a positive open for Corning.

John uses this sensitive information to his advantage. Sales traders often leak proprietary information to garner more trading activity. He's been conditioned to do whatever it takes to generate more sales, even if it means betraying his firm's position.

Click—the line noise returns.

"Al," John responds amidst a sea of voices yelling in the background.

"Yeah, I'm here, John."

"Lookin' strong at the open, ten-forty by fifty, whatcha got?"

When John says, "Lookin' strong at the open," using plain language, he leaks pre-market order flow coming across the trading desk—he's giving me the inside scoop. Information is my currency—it's the differentiating factor for why a client like Tony chooses to place Jack's order with us. He calls to get a first look at how the stock will likely perform once the market officially opens.

"Hang on."

Click—I mute John's line to talk to Tony, anonymously.

"Tony, stock's moving higher at the open, what's your interest?" I ask, informing him of the pre-market trade flow direction. *Mission accomplished.*

"Jack's lookin' to add another hundo, what's your offer mate?"

"Ten fifty-six," I reply, intuitively marking up the trade to include a bigger selling concession. In addition to my commission, I'll also share from the bid/ask spread with the trading desk. The transaction, known as a net trade with markup, generates a twelve-thousand-dollar commission.

"Brilliant, you guys are all the same," complains Tony. "At least Goldman gives us decent allocations before ripping our faces off," he says, implying that Goldman Sachs offers more shares of hot IPOs. They do; everyone on Wall Street is tired of getting their asses kicked by Goldman Sachs. They're the eight-hundred-pound gorilla that dominates the new issue market. Tony's also subtly nudging me, informing me he's already traded with them. He's undoubtedly been offered a better price on the shares I'm about to sell him.

"Jack's still gone mad over Broadcom, bullocks! What'd we get, two thousand shares on that deal? Wankers!" I take his unrelenting verbal tirade. He's a big client, making sure I know where I stand in the pecking order. I've learned not to take such comments personally.

"So, we're done?" I assume the close, knowing he's going to trade regardless of the price I've offered.

"Yeah, mate." Tony's voice calms as the end to our pre-market skirmish draws near.

"Offer hundo glowworm ten-fifty-six open." I confirm the order.

"Do it," Tony concedes the loss.

"Hang on."

Click—noise returns.

"Hey, John, hundo glowworm bid ten-fifty," I place the order.

"Got it," confirms John. He stands up, shouting across the trading floor, "Danny, hundo glowworm bid ten-fitty."

"Done, ten-fitty," Danny shouts, confirming the trade's execution.

"Done at ten-fifty," John confirms with me.

Click—I mute John's line before adding my markup, "You're done at ten-fifty-six. My best to Jack, okay?" I say calmly.

"Sure, mate, I'll let 'im know that you guys still suck! Just make sure you allocate to the offshore accounts this time—Jack's not forgotten about PentaCom."

Details matter. Even the smallest mistake can have punishing consequences. The SEC requires investors to disclose their holdings if their ownership exceeds five percent of a company's total outstanding shares. Known as a Schedule 13D filing, this document publicly discloses who controls large positions. Allocating shares across multiple offshore accounts protects Jack's holdings from the prying eyes of US regulators.

Jack recently sought a controlling interest in PentaCom stock when a clerk allocated shares to a single account. This triggered a mandatory Schedule 13D filing, disclosing his position before the company was acquired by tech giant Cisco Systems. The disclosure sent the stock soaring, and the clerical error cost Jack over ten million dollars!

We consummate the million-dollar transaction in less than two minutes. The market doesn't open for another hour, and I've already made twelve grand! Most brokers in the country are still in bed. The intoxicating effects from the power trip lingers for about thirty seconds before I'm already wondering where I'm going to come up with the rest of the $30,000 I need to pay our family's credit card bills.

Chapter 4:

Doubt Machine

If you would be a real seeker after truth, it is necessary that at least once in your life you doubt, as far as possible, all things.

—René Descartes

September 11, 2001: New York City, 8:34 a.m.

I'm watching Rick Santelli on the TV screen hanging from the wall of our trading desk. Rick's broadcasting live from the floor of the Chicago Board of Trade, where we watch news impacting the future's markets every morning.

Rick carries on, talking about recent Federal Reserve activity, as well as the jobs report data from last week. S&P Futures indicate up six points, but I already know where my clients' stock is going to open. It feels powerful to know the future before it happens—though nothing could've prepared me for what was about to happen next.

"Rick's going to commercial break. Then, it's back to the brain, David Faber, for a rundown of Nokia's earnings report," drones the television commentator.

"What's up? Uhhh, well . . . Nokia's up. After revenue growth, not as anticipated, it would appear as though the market was perhaps expecting worse news," says David.

The cable news channel CNBC is always on during trading hours. Its popular morning show *Squawk Box* is a reference to a small wooden box containing a single speaker and volume control. The squawk box is part of a closed-circuit communications network connecting Wall Street trading desks to their satellite offices around the nation. They broadcast time-sensitive information, such as analyst reports, company earnings, and other breaking news.

There's also a more covert function of squawk boxes. Their discreet, real-time communications contain non-public order flow that can be used in a regulatory gray area where stocks are traded anonymously. They work by helping trading desks identify internal (a.k.a., organic or natural) buyers and sellers. Clients interested in buying or selling very large positions are matched together in a private transaction. This "match-making" service is a common practice of large Wall Street firms where the transaction is known as a "cross trade".

Cross trades are executed in what's known as a "dark pool". Because the securities are traded privately, they're exempt from the normal reporting requirements mandated by the regulators of public exchanges. Technically, the transactions aren't illegal, they're just not reported publicly: a gray area.

Our insatiable appetite for information is fed by a steady diet of real-time financial news and unrelenting trade flows throughout the day.

David Faber is talking about American Airlines stock. "UBS has raised their price target, even though the company recently announced a 2.3-billion-dollar loss," he says.

8:50 a.m.

After the commercial break, the CNBC commentator breaks in with news, interrupting a fund manager from Oakmark.

"I'm sorry, I'm gonna interrupt you right now. We have a, uhhh, what appears to be a . . . is that the World Trade Center tower?"

A horrific scene appears on the screen that I'll never forget: the World Trade Center on fire. Gray smoke billows from a black hole, a silhouette in the shape of an aircraft etched in the side of the North Tower.

"Yeah," someone mutters from behind the scenes. "It looks like, uh . . . a plane hit it?"

"Yeah, they think so." There was more behind-the-scenes murmuring.

"This is one of the towers at the World Trade Center in Manhattan."

Really? Standing up from the trading desk, I walk over to the window to observe what's happening. A crowd of people form a row of spectators along the south-facing side of the office building. Floor-to-ceiling glass windows provide a perfect bird's-eye view of the carnage in lower Manhattan. We silently watch the surreal scene unfolding. I'm speechless as something worse than a hundred Hollywood-inspired Godzilla movies plays out before our eyes.

I don't know how long I stand there, mouth agape with no words coming out. It doesn't seem real. Suddenly, I glimpse an orange and red flash, witnessing a fireball explode through the southeastern side of the South Tower as the second plane hits.

"Oh my God!" gasps a woman's voice. Her high-pitched, broken shrill stands out amidst a macabre chorus now rising from the crowd of spectators. It's horrific. Words can't describe the sound I hear. I imagine it's the sound one makes upon learning unexpectedly of the death of their spouse or child.

The morbid memory of that sound is etched eternally in my conscious. It's the sound of fear, doubt, and uncertainty. It's the sound of the returning rumble monster, and it's paralyzing. Standing in awe of the horrific scene before me, I hear the droning sound of emergency warning sirens arise from deep within. The rumble monster roars. My subconscious kicks in, and "I'm Outta Here" comes to the rescue.

The uncomfortable feeling lasts only a moment, and then it's gone. I'm fearless.

"We're clearly not going anywhere soon, guys," I flatly announce without emotion, the rumble monster remaining safely contained in its dark cave. I'm not about to let that fearful beast out to see the light of day. "I'm gonna go grab some pizzas for the office. Who wants to go with me?" My fearless existence had no room for feelings. The brilliant red color of passion had long-since faded with the annihilation of fear.

Emotions are indiscriminate; I can't rid myself of the undesirable ones only to feel the good ones. I'd defeated the rumble monster of fear, exchanging the emotion for a learned survival instinct called fearlessness, but fearlessness comes at a price. I fail to see that suppressed fear inadvertently diminishes my fiery-red passion for life. Suppression is like a toxic bleach, whitewashing all emotions, bleeding the color out of life as excitement fades into pale complacency. This monochromatic existence is functional, but it exacts a toll on the psyche. In its wake, fearlessness leaves me numb, unable to feel anything deeply.

The same emotional process of suppression works its way through all the so-called negative emotions. When the green monster of jealousy, greed, and envy rears its ugly head, I douse it with cold, sanitizing, emotionless bleach. Unwittingly, the bright-yellow-sunlight feelings of joy and happiness fade into the sunset.

Ding, ding—the elevator bell buzzes softly and the doors open with a clunk. I make my way down the gray slate hallway of the familiar lobby at 450 Lexington Avenue. Pushing through the revolving door with a brushing whoosh sound, I'm confronted by an even more frightening scene. Witnessing the instantaneous death of a thousand people from five miles away had fractured something in my psyche. The foundation of emotional certainty I'd built my life upon cracks and shudders violently.

Walking onto the surreal scene on Lexington Avenue, I'm suddenly confronted with an alarming revelation. With the memory of the South Tower blown apart, I begin to feel something—an unfamiliar sensation. *Is this what a feeling actually feels like?* My subconscious wonders.

I don't recognize the sensation at first. I'd read about feelings before, I'd seen actors portray feelings in movies, but I can't say I've ever distinguished my own sensations as feelings. It's the feeling of being alive!

With the small, safe container I'd lived inside now blown apart, my numb, fearless existence begins to thaw: a surprise gift I didn't want, a white elephant. A sensation so real and visceral washes over me as something asleep inside begins to stir. The experience pierces my soul, and the container that holds my heart enlarges. I feel like the Grinch in Dr. Seuss's *How the Grinch Stole Christmas*:

Well . . . in Whoville they say
That the Grinch's small heart
Grew three sizes that day!
And then, the true meaning of Christmas came through
And the Grinch found the strength of ten Grinches, plus two.

There isn't a single car on the normally bustling avenue. A crowd of ashen zombies shuffle their way up Lexington, covered in dust from the towers' collapse. As far as the eye can see, disorganized groups circle around portable radios in the middle of the street, their only connection to what's happening.

The cataclysmic event exposes the inner workings of the Wall Street apparatus for what it is; the ghost in the machine reveals itself as the apparition of fear and doubt. It's been said that Wall Street is driven by fear and greed. I've learned that greed is simply another side of fear. Doubt lies at the heart of it all. I'm afraid I'll lose what I have, and I'm afraid I won't get what I want. Fear resides on both sides of the same coin; it's all doubt. Doubt is the currency of Wall Street.

Long before the ramparts of lower Manhattan were erected, Descartes understood the mathematics of the doubt machine. His work remains at the forefront of the debate surrounding human consciousness today. "*Cogito, ergo sum*: I think, therefore I am." The answer to the question "Who am I?" identifies itself in doubt, uncertainty. If we exist because of our thoughts, and our most basic reasoning is rooted in doubt and fear, then this is the shaky foundation of our reality.

Like any machine, the doubt machine requires fuel. Its consumers provide an endless supply. The entire system functions elegantly in a natural symbiotic relationship. Fueled by fear, we seek certainty. The question "Who am I?" arises in consciousness, and uncertainty is the inevitable answer. The more we seek certainty, the more we generate uncertainty.

The machine works through a dreadful algorithm: an optimization protocol seeking to resolve questions without answers. The simplified version of the formula is this:

$$\text{fear} + \text{desire for certainty} = \text{uncertainty}$$

Did I make the right decision, or the wrong decision? Will I make money, or lose money? Was that a good idea, or a bad idea? Did I succeed or fail, win or lose? What's going to happen next? We're all driven mad by uncertainty, terrified we'll get the wrong answer. The calculus in the sum of all fears is represented by a single equation. The doubt machine searches for a binary result from the basic question: buy or sell? It's the most efficient machine ever devised by the conscious mind, and its answer is uncertain.

The moment a decision is made to buy or sell, an alchemical reaction is released in our minds. The result feeds the machine. Fear and doubt occur simultaneously in a synthesis of uncertainty. Seeking immortality from fear, we drink from the Holy Grail—the imagined certainty of controlling our fate in the markets. Instead, we find it contains a witch's brew—a hemlock! The machine goes to work with deadly precision. Carried upon electromagnetic waves, uncertainty emanates from an energetic source deep in the cavernous bedrock of Lower Manhattan. From subterranean depths, the rumbling monster churns out new products for insatiable consumers each day.

In the wake of the 9/11 attacks, I experience a growing awareness of the presence of the *not-good*. I'd first felt its sinister energy in 1974 as a two-year-old. As I grew up, life seemed somehow determined by fate. As an adult, I knew I'd played an important role as the agent of choice. Setting my sights on the prize of "certainty," I'd found the solution: the ancient Chinese proverb, "Be careful what you wish for, lest it come true," a self-fulfilling prophecy. I had the wealth, health, and family I wanted, won (in part) one sale at a time, by choice after choice in order to keep fear and doubt at bay. I'd conditioned myself not to react to emotions; they cloud judgement. Feelings are an unwelcomed intrusion. Emotions interfere with rational thought; it's better to not acknowledge them than risk making a wrong deci-sion. I'd become a risk manager, creating a safe, predictable, and small life. I'd become fearlessly unaware.

The divine spark I'd sought had found me. It'd always been there, but in the wake of disaster, I felt it. I remembered my future. Outside of space and time, a date with divinity called out from eternity. The spark ignited something. Emerging from the smoldering ashes of the World Trade Center, a distant light of hope was born.

What's this feeling? Searching for answers from the oracle of Wall Street, the doubt machine leaves me with only more uncertainty.

I was desperately in need of an intervention, and I didn't even know it.

Who am I?

PART TWO: ABYSS

Chapter 5:

Divine Intervention

The most difficult question in theology is this: Why does God allow evil? If God is all-good and all-power-ful, then why are our lives marked with pain and suffering? These are not abstract questions. They go right to the heart of our experience. We have each wrestled with misery, wondering when God would intervene.

—Bishop Robert Barron

March 2007: Princeton, New Jersey

"I want to go to the park," Ashley exclaims with child-like inno-cence. She's my seven-year-old, the most angelic being on the planet. "Biscuit!" she gleefully shouts, grinning from ear to ear. Our dog, Biscuit, comes bounding around the corner. Doggy toes designed to dig into soft soil bounce clickety-clack off the polished hardwood floor of our home in Princeton, New Jersey. Sliding across the floor, Biscuit attempts a courageous leap through the air, landing squarely in Ashley's welcoming arms. "Biscuit, you're the best little doggy ever!" Ashley giggles. Biscuit's pink tummy flashes as he love-tackles her, slobbering soft wet kisses over her glowing pale face. It's one of those perfect early-spring mornings in the Northeast. Remnants of a late-winter storm linger. Swiftly melting globs of white slush slide from conifers laden with heavy, wet snow. Outside my base-ment office window, random sloshy notes erupt in an impressive symphony of nature, interrupting the peaceful morning.

"Okay, okay, Ashley. Geez, ten minutes," I call out from behind a pair of glowing computer screens. Working for a Wall Street financed startup in 2007 has its perks, but everything comes with a price. Uninterrupted weekends with the family are rare. My hands tremble. I'm bleary-eyed from the previous evening, when I'd overin-dulged in an opulent cabernet from a fraternity brothers' vineyard in California. The fading but distinct smell of fine red wine leaks from my pores.

"Hurry up, Dad," Ashley insists. "Biscuit needs to go for a walk!"

"I told you, ten minutes!" I bark in response. "I'll be right there. Chill out, little angel." Angelic she is. Pure, carefree, innocent . . . well, okay, not exactly innocent. We never censor anything she watches on TV, and God only knows what she's seen on the internet. She's growing up way too fast, seeing way too much. In other words, she's experiencing a pretty average childhood in the shadowy urban sprawl surrounding Gotham City, New York. Little do I know how prophetic my little angel's soft voice will become.

Locking Ashley into place, the seatbelt clicks in affirmation. I jump into the driver's seat and speed off. A looming three o'clock deadline approaches: a rendezvous with my company's CEO. He awaits a briefing I've prepared for a second round of investor meetings. But this is our family time, which means it is time to switch gears. Fumbling for my seatbelt, I attempt to drive one-handed, swerving into the oncoming lane. Just then, the shoulder harness jams.

"Fuck!" I proclaim out loud, jerking the steering wheel hard.

"That's not right!" Ashley shouts from the back seat. Completely unfazed by my profane outburst, she's genuinely concerned for my safety. "Put your seatbelt on, Dad!"

Ignoring her protests, I speed past her objection and into the unforgettable morning. Biscuit bounds around the Delaware-Raritan Canal Trail. Less than a five-minute drive from home, Carnegie Lake is dog heaven. Splashing and trouncing, he frolics through the muddy gravel edges lining the thin path wrapped around the lake. He's promptly covered from head to toe with little twigs and leaves, dirt and pond scum.

"Great," I mutter sarcastically under my breath. I know it'll be my job to bathe him upon our return home. Though Biscuit clearly enjoys frolicking in pond scum, it'll be trench warfare to sell him on getting into a bathtub.

"Biscuit's shivering, Dad, let's go home!" Ashley squeals as our family time comes to an end. I race home, bathe the protesting dog, and speed off again into Princeton. I'm right on time for my date with divinity.

That's not right! Ashley's premonition rings in my ears as I wait for the traffic light to turn green. As I wait, I reflect on the success that's led to this moment, imagining a future that's sure to follow. I'd grasped the momentum, taken the bull by the horns. It feels powerful taking charge of my own destiny—a self-fulfilling prophecy of success. I attribute my success to hard work, ambitions born out of my own hand. I've arrived; there are no limits to my success. I'm the youngest partner of our company's most promising new venture, a billion-dollar multi-family office. We're on the verge of creating vast fortunes for all involved. The stock market's making new highs, and the wind's at our back. *I'm going to have it all!* I'm living the American dream. I've invested nearly ten years climbing the corporate ladder before launching into the thin atmosphere of entrepreneurship. I wait expectantly for my golden parachute to open. It'd be eight more years before that'd happen—just long enough to hit rock bottom before deploying.

There's always been a small place for God in my large life, but the miniscule space allotted to spiritual growth is crowded by the necessities of life. My neoclassic virtues are dictated by a survival of the fittest mentality. I live a Darwinist reality, centered on choice and personal responsibility. Of course, there'll be collateral damage; we need only observe nature to see the casualties surrounding us. It's obviously a dog-eat-dog world, and you eat what you kill.

Ayn Rand's objectivist twist on Polonius's quote in Hamlet, "to thine own self be true," serves as my guide. When I was eighteen, I'd read her classic, *The Fountainhead*. Her philosophy of objectivism, based on the four pillars of reality, reason, self-interest, and capitalism, shaped my worldview and carried me upon waves of personal success. When personal achievement and my own happiness served as the sole purpose of my life, objectivism contained everything I needed to achieve results. Rand summarizes her philosophy in the following quote:

> *My philosophy, in essence, is the concept of man as a heroic being, with his own happiness as the moral purpose of his life, with productive achievement as his noblest activity, and reason as his only absolute.*

> —*Ayn Rand, Atlas Shrugged*

I felt sorry for those unfortunates possessing a lesser intellect, misguided by what they call morality. Rational self-interest, leading to personal responsibility, was the only moral code I needed. It took the intervention of a numinous power to expand my consciousness beyond the limiting beliefs of a purely rational-minded objectivist. Religious family members would later proclaim that "God had a different plan for my life." I tend to agree; something more meaningful than visions of grandeur dreamt up in a Wall Street boardroom lay ahead. "For what does it profit a man to gain the whole world and forfeit his soul?" (Mark 8:36) The providence of "God's will, not mine be done" would soon be self-evident. His ransom price: nothing short of the life I'd been living.

***

That's not right, Dad. Put your seatbelt on! Ashley's message echoes again in my head. Her warning prompts me to reach over and attempt to untangle the frozen seat belt. Yanking, I jerk the shoulder belt free from its stuck position and then secure it with a *click*. Speeding along the Princeton-Kingston Highway, I contemplate my past, present, and future—the glorious life I'd been personally responsible for creating. Without a cloud in the sky, I'm grateful for the rewards of my labor: my beautiful daughter, my wife, my home, my cars, my retirement accounts, my health, my purposeful job. I'm well on my way to having it all. Come to think of it, I already have it all. The only limit is the limit of human imagination. I'm propelled towards more, more, more! There's so much more to be gained in this life; besides, no one can say for certain whether an afterlife even exists.

Imagining what my "more" looks like, I drift into a blissful daydream. Heaven on earth includes: a more accommodating home with a gourmet kitchen, marbled spa rooms, a media room, and an outdoor fire pit for entertaining guests. I envision a Land Rover and a Mercedes with my own driver and fractional ownership of a private jet to shuttle us on eco-vacations to exotic locations. I want a hedge-fund-sized retirement account, and an ivy-league-sized education account—trust funds and insurance policies to protect my wife, daughter, and unborn grandchildren. I want a family foundation reflecting contemporary philanthropic values, and a museum-quality fine art collection. Lastly, I'd make contributions to the church—an obliged afterthought that I'm almost embarrassed to admit. On second thought, friends and coworkers pursuing their own objectivist ends might disapprove; spiritual, not religious, would be the politically correct ideal to uphold. It would be better to commission the building of a public meditation center and not risk offending anyone.

I envision so much more, more, more! Materialist ambitions dominate my thoughts. Cloaked in the ideals and values of a progressive New York elite, I imagine someday I'll be initiated into their exclusive club. There's no limit to my desire. Contemporary Western culture doesn't appear to have evolved much. Vanity and self-centered ambition masquerade as charity and virtue. Far from being virtuous, my values more closely resemble Daffy Duck in the 1957 cartoon *Ali Baba Bunny*: "It's mine, you understand? Mine! All mine! Get back in there! Down, down, down! Go, go, go! Mine, mine, mine! Mwa-ha-ha-ha!"

I approach the notorious speed trap at the intersection of Mercer and Nassau. Slowing the car to 35 mph, the light ahead is green as

I pass through the intersection. Suddenly, I glimpse something blur into my peripheral vision. With only microseconds of reaction time, I slam the brakes. Squealing into the middle of the intersection, my car collides into the side of a Honda Odyssey minivan filled with small children. It's a moment of divine intervention, a date with divinity. My right knee explodes into the dashboard, instantly shattering into a thousand pieces. The shoulder harness holds as my face plants firmly into the deploying airbag. The cabin clouds over with a fine powder.

***

"You okay, dude?" comes the voice of a twenty-something-year-old kid through the dusty cabin. He'd witnessed the accident and helps me out of the car and onto the curb. The ambulance ride and time in the emergency room are a blur. I remember my relief to learn that the children and driver of the minivan were unharmed. Thank God I was the only one who sustained injuries from the crash.

The extent to which this divine intervention impacts my life's path is profound; it's a watershed event, and a tipping point in the universe was met. A centrifugal force ripples from the epicenter of the car's impact, altering my life's course. It's a gift, and like many others who've received such gifts from above (or within, depending on your leanings), today I recognize that God did for me what I could not do for myself. There'd be further gifts in store for my uncertain future. Sometimes I wish God would've kept some of these gifts, but that would've made quite a different story, and a very different life. The one I've been blessed with today is far better than anything I could have imagined for myself.

The ambulance pulls into the emergency room bay at the hospital. I'm in a lot of pain, and my knee is throbbing. "X-rays reveal a stellate fracture of the right patella," says the emergency room radiologist.

"Speak English please, doc."

"Your knee exploded."

"Thanks."

"You're going to require surgery right away. I hope you know a good orthopedist?"

I start to pray, perhaps for the first time in my life, an earnest prayer. It went something like this: "God, help me. I know you're the God of healing and all, but what I really need right now is a great fucking doctor. Thanks."

I was moving away from objectivism and toward some form of faith. It was a beginning.

Chapter 6:

Doctor God

"I have an M.D. from Harvard, I am board certified in cardio-thoracic medicine and trauma surgery, I have been awarded citations from seven different medical boards in New England, and I am never, ever sick at sea."

"You ask me if I have a God complex? Let me tell you something: I am God."

—Doctor Jed Hill, Malice (1993 film)

May 2007: Princeton, New Jersey
Doctor God: Part One

"You're recovering remarkably well, considering surgery was just six weeks ago," beams my orthopedic surgeon. Doctor God smiles in appreciation, admiring the results of his life's work. Harvard-educated and physician to the US Olympic rowing team, Doctor God's an accomplished orthopedic surgeon. The trust I place in him is unconditional. Some consider him to be the best orthopedic surgeon in New Jersey. The US Olympic rowing team considers him an actual God—a Doctor God. Based on his results, I'm not sure their faith in him is misplaced.

"I'm tempted to discharge you from my care, but before I do, I should ask if you've been experiencing any further symptoms?"

"Well, now that you mention it, I do have this peculiar tremor in my right thumb." Having been granted an audience with Doctor God, I'm going to milk it for all it's worth! "I'm stressed the fuck out, Doc. I've been shoutin' on phones, hammerin' keys and watchin' news feeds." I continue at my usual frenetic pace. "I mean seriously, I'm dealin' in stocks, bonds, currencies, options, and derivatives—it's like running ten hedge funds! I'm jugglin' four screens with five lines on hold." I rattle on without taking a breath. "Half the time I don't know if I'm even married anymore. Hell, my shrink tells me I'm married to my Bloomberg terminal! It's 24/7 client bullshit. I need a drink and a quick decision!"

I'm still speaking rapid-fire-New-York fast—the language I'd learned while investing and spending over a decade as a Wall Street slave to greed and ambition. "Probably just carpal tunnel, huh? Maybe stress? I just read 'bout something called RSI—repetitive strain injury, I think they call it. I don't know, you're the doc, what's the story? Shoot me straight!"

In typical type-A fashion, I expectantly await his validation of my best self-diagnosis: carpal tunnel syndrome. After all, Doctor God's considered *the best* orthopedist—who better to confirm what the hell this pesky little tremor's all about? I hadn't really put much thought into it; I was way too busy to bother.

"Hmmm," mumbles the good doctor. "Peculiar indeed. Considering you were in a car accident that damaged your knee, let's take closer look."

Gently taking my right arm into his skilled hands, he manipulates my thumb, then wrist, then elbow, before concluding his brief survey by rotating my shoulder. His expression promptly shifts out of character. That radiant bright glow of pride from yet another job well done reverses to a ghostly pale-gray shade. His typical jocular demeanor, that hallmark trait shared by a fraternity of East Coast professionals, is replaced with an almost reverent, deeply troubled disposition.

"You'd better get in to see a neurologist right away. My secretary will get you a referral if you need one."

His delivery seems nearly rehearsed. There must be a Harvard class where prospective doctors learn bedside manners on how to deliver *bad news*. Deliberate, precise, clinical. Like that of a military casualty notification officer dutifully pronouncing the death of a loved one, his sullen expression betrays a lurking confession being withheld.

Clearly, he sees something, but what is it? Why's he withholding infor-mation? I sense the predicament he's confronted by. With impeccable professionalism, he intuitively knows he's not qualified to make such a serious diagnosis, even though what he thinks is readily apparent.

No, this kind of bad news must be delivered by an appropriately qualified adjudicator—a skilled neurologist.

***

The next twenty-four hours crawl by at a snail's pace. I call in a favor to secure an immediate appointment with a local neurologist. No small feat, as even the average ones are booked solid for three months. The next day, my wife and I timidly walk up to the 1970s-fashioned complex of doctors' offices to hear the judge render his official verdict.

"You have Parkinson's disease," he says flatly. With no bedside manner at all, Doctor not-God delivers the fatal blow, revealing his not-Harvard medical school qualifications. An indescribable sense of fear and dread descends. The rumble monster returns with a vengeance. I'm stunned, shell-shocked, and everything goes numb. The world blurs as life begins to move in slow motion. I fall into a dream-like trance and become the observer of my life, having an out-of-body experience.

Frame-by-frame, I see the gavel fall in slow motion. I've received a lifetime sentence, destined to live in a progressively decaying body without chance for pardon or parole. *Who am I?* asks a scared, uncertain voice. The future alters course in a microsecond. My certain future based upon hopeful dreams and ambitions is suddenly replaced with uncertainty. One thing I'm certain of is that someday I'll be huddled in a corner, shaking uncontrollably with drool spilling out the side of my mouth. Nobody will want to have anything to do with me. That's where I'll be spending my retirement.

In a flash, I go from being on top of the world to being . . . *I don't know what*, but I do know it's *not-good*. I'll never forget sitting in the parking lot with my sobbing wife. I suppose our response could be characterized as denial.

"It's just not possible, Alex. You're only thirty-four, and you're one of the healthiest people I know. You eat *tofu*, for God's sake! How could you possibly have Parkinson's disease? We need a second opinion." I agree; we need an appropriately credentialed doctor to render a verdict that comes with a lifetime sentence. Another Doctor God is called in.

Doctor God: Part Two

Considered by many to be *the best* neurologist on the planet, the next Doctor God I seek is a rare find in the world of medicine. He's both department head of neurology at Mount Sinai Hospital and chairman emeritus of neuroscience at Columbia University. Balancing research at the highest level while serving in a clinical practice, he's without equal in his field. There's no limit to what he's capable of! It's been rumored that he's treated such high-profile individuals as former attorney general Janet Reno and Pope John Paul II. He's a real Doctor God that even the Pope trusts his life to! This is one judge with whom there'd be no contest.

"Neurology," says a street-smart voice at the other end of the phone.

"Yes, I'd like to make an appointment for an initial consult with Doctor God."

"I'm sorry, but Doctor God isn't taking new patients at this time," replies the young woman.

"Yes, but my attorney is an existing patient of his," I hurriedly reply. "He suggested I call for the initial consult. Wouldn't you just be so kind and put me through to the person responsible for his calendar?"

"Who's your attorney?" she asks skeptically. I respond with his name. "One moment."

Click, the phone is transferred . . . ringing.

"Neurology," answers a voice in a heavy Brooklyn accent.

"Hello, yes? Uhhh," I stutter before recovering my confident voice. "My attorney is an existing patient of Doctor God's. He suggested I call for an initial consultation?"

"I don't think he's takin' new patients right now. Who'd ya say referred ya?"

Skilled at handling professional gatekeepers, a few more namedrops open the gate.

"Doctor God's next available appointment is six months out. He's teachin' twice a week and only shows up here on Wednesdays when he's not out at the college doin' work."

I secure a two-hour appointment, and I'm told that I'll meet with the doctor for fifteen minutes. This is how the Doctor Gods practice their trade; they see you when they see you, if they see you at all. I'm granted an audience with the king for fifteen minutes. The rest of the time, I'd be treated by an army of twenty-something-year-old fellows and interns.

The next six months feel like an eternity. Finally, I'm in front of Doctor God, waiting for him to bestow his wisdom. "Early-Onset Parkinson's Disease [EOPD] typically progresses more slowly than the kind of Parkinson's that generally afflicts people over the age of sixty," says Doctor God, choosing words with precision before handing me off to one of his fellows for further treatment. The fellow promptly writes me a prescription for a drug produced by a pharmaceutical company that generously donates to the Columbia Department of Neuroscience.

It takes less than a year for my new reality to set in: I'm thirty-five years old, and I have Parkinson's disease. There's no denying it, though my wife and I try our best to. Inside of six months, we're divorcing.

I respond in typical fashion: "I'll have another," I slur. It's the third round of martinis at *Lahier's*, the iconic French restaurant in Princeton that'll become one of my many haunts. *This had to be the bottom*, I thought. Little did I know it was going to get much, much, worse before it would get any better.

I need a hope and a prayer, but both elude me. Evangelists call it a "backslide." I'm restless, irritable, and discontent, searching for what alcoholics describe as "that sense of ease and comfort that comes at once by taking a few drinks." From this downtrodden state, I evoke the universal prayer of desperation: "My God, I need another drink!"

Two hours later, I'm stumbling into the night. Driving home, I wonder: *Who am I?*

Chapter 7:

Haunted Houses

There appears to be a conscience in mankind which severely punishes the man who does not somehow and at some time, at whatever cost to his pride, cease to defend and assert himself, and instead confess himself fallible and human.

—Carl Gustav Jung

October 2010: Princeton, New Jersey

"Another one?" Joe, the bartender, smiles. Soft around the middle, he's portly and balding. I'd guess he's in his late thirties. With a ruddy complexion and the hint of an Irish accent, Joe's a true friend—as far as bartenders go. I really don't know two things about him, though we've spent enough time together to be family.

Little chunks of ice slide down the frozen pint glass of a Coors Light he sets down in front of me. Tiny golden bubbles glimmer hopefully in the dim cellar barroom. Crawling up the side of the pint, a frothy head emerges, spilling out over the mighty mahogany bar.

"Colorado champagne," Joe chuckles in his familiar, comforting tone. "It's Halloween, Al, anything worth celebrating?"

It's happy hour. I unhappily find myself at my usual seat at the Yankee Doodle Tap Room in the Nassau Inn at Palmers Square in Princeton. I can't think of anything remotely worth celebrating. Wiping dripping beer foam from the frothy head, I make a crude New Jersey joke: "You do give good head, Joe! That's worth a celebration."

Chuckling, Joe asks, "Chicken wings or burger tonight?"

"I'm really not that hungry. Can you box up a burger to go? I think I'm gonna head home early and get some work done."

"Yeah right, sure thing, Al," Joe says, skeptically. Seven minutes later, he pushes a Styrofoam box towards me. Inside is the charred remains of a burnt cow sitting on a hard roll. Plastic cups of red ketchup and a pile of greasy fries leak out the side of the to-go box.

The pint glass, still cold in my hands, is nearing empty.

"One more for the road?" Joe asks.

"Nah, I already closed out my tab. I'm gonna go ahead and get outta here," I mutter unconvincingly.

"On me!" Joe chirps merrily. The third pint of the night clacks down onto the heavily shellacked bar. Joe sweeps a damp, gray rag across the dull mahogany finish, worn out by years of persistent use. The distinct scent of lemon pledge, stale beer, and Marlborough cigarettes kicks up into the dank air.

"Thanks, Joe." I half-smile in complacent approval. Such is the ritual attitude of denial. "When you gonna let me buy you a drink sometime?" I offer.

"I don't drink," Joe flatly replies.

"Oh yeah, I forgot."

If you only had my problems, you'd drink too, whispers a silent, diabolical voice deep in my subconscious.

Joe's the best bartender in town. *Why is it that the best bartenders don't drink?* I wonder through a melancholy haze as my beer buzz starts to pick up. *People at their best rarely drink.* Silently, I loathe Joe's cheerful attitude and professional aptitude. Pessimism dominates my thinking. Tossing an extra five bucks onto the bar, I march into the cold October evening. The autopilot kicks on. Conditioned by months of an all-too-familiar routine, I stumble past Lacy Silhouettes Lingerie, a high-end intimate clothing boutique. I climb the stairs to my tomb at 31 Palmer Square West, above Thomas Sweet Chocolates, a local favorite of Princeton University students. I've selected the apartment based on its location, equidistant between my office at 34 Hulfish and the old tavern. My commute from home to the tavern is the distance I can strike a seven iron: a convenience that enables a ready cure for my self-diagnosed condition known as a "wicked vodka deficiency."

Fumbling with my keys, I'm distracted by a fleeting memory of a sign I'd just seen in the window of the boutique lingerie store:

"Two-for-one wedding negligees." I turn that one over a few times in my head, trying to comprehend the logic. The old apartment key grinds around the tumblers of a rusty lock. Shuffling inside, I kick the creaking door closed behind me. Hands grapple an armload of unfinished paperwork as the door slams shut with a loud clunk.

I'm not drunk, I tell myself, *more like heavily buzzed. I have nowhere to drive, and nowhere to be tonight. I'm drinking responsibly.* Subconscious denial serves my need for permission as I blindly search for the familiar remedy to my problems. *Time to get this job done right,* says an unspoken, diabolic voice. Out comes the slumbering vodka jug from its frozen crypt in the galley kitchen of the tiny apartment overlooking the square. Skeletons in the closet anesthetize me, and the nightmare ritual of oblivion begins again.

Pavlov, meet Popov. It can't be good when you've resorted to drinking bad vodka from a plastic jug alone on a Tuesday work night. My weak body collapses onto a hard, wooden chair and I sit in silence, stewing at my kitchen table. Through the open screened window, I hear a group of teenagers swearing at each other on the street below.

Sweeping my thumb past a biometric authentication pad, the Bloomberg springs to life. Glowing computer displays illuminate the dark room with scrolling news stories. Asian currency markets light up blood red—a premonition of the market's open in New York. I cautiously watch as the Bank of Japan's (BOJ) release of economic data assaults the Asian markets. The dancing numbers intensify, foretelling the outcome of a desperate era of monetary policy. Abenomics (a.k.a., QE, quantitative easing) is a failed BOJ monetary policy originally attempted in 2001. The failed policy would soon be in full swing in the United States. Resurrected by Ben Bernanke and the Federal Reserve, QE is a desperate measure intended to block the bloodthirsty, vampiric short-sellers and shore up dysfunctional credit markets. It's a futile attempt to resuscitate the dying patient, a failing US economy suffering cardiac arrest: the unintended consequence of zero-rate policy decisions.

I've just concluded a review of our investor's portfolios, anticipating the impact that QE will have on their cash investments. A billion dollars of private wealth demands to know why the fees we charge exceed the interest earned on their $400-million *risk-free* treasury portfolio. The result of my analysis? Our decision to invest in risk-free T-bills is generating negative returns!

"We don't pay you to lose money—we know how to do that just fine on our own" would undoubtedly be our clients' response to my efforts to protect their wealth. Financial markets are collapsing on the back of a crisis rivaling the great depression, and our company is on the verge of failure. *This has to be the bottom.* Starting from what I'd perceived as the pinnacle of success, in just under eighteen months, I'd lost everything. I take inventory, accounting for my losses.

PERSONAL LOSS INVENTORY:

- I've lost my marriage, custody of my daughter, and my house.

- I've lost my health, my mind, and I'm fifty
pounds overweight.

- Rent's due in less than a week, and I'm late on monthly
support obligations.

- I owe the Internal Revenue Service $120,000, and the Visa
company $50,000.

- I've agreed to a nine-year, half-a-million-dollar pledge to my
ex-wife that I've no idea how to pay for.

- Lastly, I owe attorney's fees totaling nearly $30,000 because
I failed to produce documents valuing my now-worthless
partnership at the company.

  TOTAL VALUE: I'm wiped out, worthless, a complete annihilation!

All told, the divorce cost over a million dollars. I have more than just a feeling of being worthless; I *am* worthless! *Your life insurance policy is worth more than you are!* Says the diabolical voice. I feel lower than ever before. "I, I, I. Me, me, me. Your 'I's' are too close together, and your 'Gods' too small" would be the cheerful response from my sponsor in Alcoholics Anonymous. That hopeful future is still years away. Presently, I'm so mired in self-pity, self-loathing, and morbid reflection that I can't get out of my own way.

"Let's face it, your life's a complete failure," says the voice of IT, keeping score in my mind.

IT's right—I am a loser. I've proven to myself that I can rise to any level, achieve whatever I set my intentions upon, and this is where my best intentions have led me. I've convinced myself there's no limit to the success I'm capable of, and now I've proven there's no limit to the devastating loss I can feel. Running on my own steam, I'm heading off the rails, a runaway train wreck. My life's unmanageable, and I'm absolutely powerless to stop any of it.

My track record with prayer isn't particularly great up to this point. Nonetheless, I persist in my faith. With unbending fortitude, I summon the Great Power once again. To date, it hasn't done dog-shit for me. Usually, I just start praying. Sometimes I get on my knees, adding to the dramatic effect, and to let God know I'm really serious! This time I'm lying prone on my hardwood floor, face planted into my hands. I'm really going for it! I don't necessarily recommend this one, and I can't recall it verbatim, but here's essentially how my abiding faith and persistent vodka dependency led my broken heart to pray that night:

Prayer of Annihilation

Holy and merciful Father, maybe I'm doing this prayer thing all wrong? You created me, and I've managed to really fuck up my life pretty good. It's a real shit-show down here, and I know I'm the one responsible for it. I've hit the wall, and it should've killed me. It didn't, and I'm pretty sure it was supposed to. Maybe you're just a figment of my imagination? Maybe you've fallen asleep? I can't seem to find any sign of hope, and I've lost my way in this darkness. I'm begging you, if there's a benevolent spirit somewhere in your forsaken universe, please summon it now and put an end to my miserable existence, mercifully. I just can't take it anymore, and I don't have the courage to do it myself. End it quickly. I love you, Jesus, Amen.

I've been through desperate times before. I've spent countless hours praying the Divine Office, but I've never found a prayer that equals the despair I feel in this despondent moment. I stumble my way to the edge of oblivion. Peering into the abyss, I'm in the presence of imminent annihilation. My prayer's heartfelt, and I mean it.

This is *the absolute bottom.*

It wasn't.

At this point in my story, I'd like to say that Jesus miraculously rode in on his white horse to save the day.

He didn't.

I prayed for the white horse, and God sent the four horsemen of the apocalypse. The bottom has a way of sinking a little lower when you're in it—a little deeper, a little darker. That's how it happened for me at least; it's the terrible gift of desperation. This God business was starting to wear thin. For some reason, I had to probe the depths of hell to find the light. I'm not sure why it worked that way for me, it just did. I guess I'll just chalk it up to "God works in mysterious ways."

I feel terrible. *Where am I?* I blindly ask in the bleak shadows of despair.

"Lost," replies a diabolic voice.

Is there anything left to do?

"Have another drink," IT says.

Halfway into the plastic Popov jug, I consider the imponderable. *Who am I?*

"Hopeless," replies the shadow.

Where am I?

"You're in the depths of despair, the abyss of annihilation."

Then it came to me. Like a lightning bolt from heaven, I knew what I had to do. In my final hours, I'd descend further into the depths of that dark abyss, return to a watery void I knew well. As the old dive saying goes, *diver down!*

Chapter 8:

Exit Strategy

On the day when the weight deadens on your shoulders and you stumble, may the clay dance to balance you. And when your eyes freeze behind the grey window and the ghost of loss gets in to you, may a flock of colors, indigo, red, green, and azure blue come to awaken in you a meadow of delight.

When the canvas frays in the currach of thought and a stain of ocean blackens beneath you, may there come across the waters a path of yellow moonlight to bring you safely home.

—John O'Donohue, "Beannacht / Blessing"

November 2010: Port Barnegat, New Jersey

"Dive, dive, dive!" barks the captain of the *Gypsy Blood*, a custom fifty-foot dive boat chartered out of Port Barnegat, New Jersey. A light snow falls in the freezing gray November air. I silently observe my dive buddy stumble aft towards a platform at the stern of the ship. He lumbers by in a trilaminate dry suit, carrying over a hundred pounds of twin steel cylinders on a halcyon backpack. Heaving the cylinders over a pair of submerged ladders, he plunges into the icy Atlantic waters with an awkward *ker-sploosh*!

Deftly maneuvering into position, his massive body displaces choppy waves. Turning to raise a thick neoprene glove above the ocean's surface, he taps the top of his hood with his fist, indicating the divers' signal for "okay."

"Ready?" the boat captain yells from the bow. "You're next Al, let's go! Dive, dive, dive!" I stand up from the flat aluminum bench, shuffling in a pair of heavy, frogman-style Jet Fin flippers to the platform edge. Wobbling awkwardly, I stretch my right flipper out. Stepping into a giant stride entry, I plunge into the dark-gray Atlantic water. Instantly, my face is assaulted with what feels like a thousand needles as forty-degree saltwater strikes the exposed skin around my dive mask. Pressing the low-pressure inflator, I completely fill my buoyancy control device (BCD) with air. Bouncing on gyrating waves, I turn to face the boat captain, repeating the "okay" ritual.

Deflating the BCD bladder, I descend into murky depths and search for my dive buddy. Twenty feet below the surface, I spot him making his way along the Carolina rig, a thick rope suspended by weights that extends from the bow to the stern of the ship. Kicking hard against the stiff current, water slowly permeates through the neoprene hood as my face acclimates to the bone-chilling temperature and my ice-cream headache diminishes.

Pulled by gravity, I begin to sink quickly. My heart races as my body picks up momentum, descending into the depths like a falling rock. I desperately reach out, flailing as I grab at the safety of the submerged rope. Thick gloves grasp the line, and I breathe in several deep sighs of relief. My heart slows to a normal rate as I hang suspended for a moment while I adjust my gear. Like a vacuum-packed freezer bag, my dry suit grips tightly around me. Hitting the chest-inflator button, the dry-suit-squeeze immediately releases, and I relax into a neutrally buoyant position.

My dive buddy awaits me at the line leading to the anchor below. We complete our final "okay" before making our first descent. Spying a bubble trail streaming off his tank valve, I clumsily fiddle with his air control valve. Five-millimeter wetsuit gloves in near-freezing Atlantic waters aren't particularly dexterous, but I manage to tighten the valve enough to eliminate the bubble stream. After giving the final "okay" sign, I follow his descent into the darkness below.

He attaches a flashing beacon to the ship's anchor on the ocean floor about sixty feet down, and then he looks for a place to connect his wreck reel. Wreck diving protocol requires a diver to spool a thin rope line from their utility belt to the ship's anchor tie-in point. In the event of strong currents or low visibility conditions, the wreck line serves as a breadcrumb trail, leading a disoriented diver back to the safety of the boat's anchor.

My dive buddy pauses to assess the half-dozen lines that've already been put down on the very small wreck area. With so many lines spaghettied all around, he surmises there'd be plenty of options to follow home. He briefly contemplates his next action before signaling he'll follow someone else's line instead of setting down his own.

I've been wreck diving for a few years, but I'm not nearly as experienced as my dive buddy. A fire fighter skilled in rescue and recovery, he's a well-respected member of our diving community. I trust his qualifications for managing virtually any underwater emergency.

The rules of wreck diving differ from that of recreational diving. In recreational settings, we're taught to never leave the side of your dive buddy. The intention is that your dive buddy will always be nearby to provide support in the event of equipment failure or other underwater emergencies.

Wreck divers are trained to manage emergencies that contemplate a more perilous set of circumstances. The confined spaces and overhead environments of sunken ships increase the risk that a dive buddy may not be accessible. Wreck divers train to use redundant equipment and assume responsibility that a dive buddy may not be able to lend aid in an emergency. I thought about all the lines tied to the anchor and reasoned there'd be plenty of divers around to help in an emergency. By choosing to follow someone else's line, I'd broken the first unspoken rule of wreck diving and its corollary:

> **Wreck-Diving Rule Number One:** When the shit hits the fan, you *are* your own dive buddy.

> **Corollary:** Never rely on someone else to save your own dumb ass.

Most New Jersey wreck divers would give their life to save another. My dive buddy's no exception. Like soldiers at war, if you're around long enough, you inevitably see people die. Wreck diving is similar, and we treat our companions with appropriate reverence. While no one's left behind, we acknowledge the reality of our decision. To wreck dive is to take your life in your own hands. Wreck divers are chivalrous, but usually not stupid. Not laying down a wreck line is just plain dumb!

It's dark, and the surging ocean churns out foggy, gray clouds of detritus, bringing visibility down to under ten feet. The familiar conditions are typical of New Jersey shore diving. I set out against the current. The theory is to swim against the current at the beginning of the dive, so you can drift back with the current at the end of it—that's the theory, at least. Experienced divers will tell you that ocean currents, especially of the surging variety, have a way of shifting mid-dive.

I begin my dive in typical fashion, looking for bugs (lobsters) on the ocean floor. They're commonly found in nooks and crannies around wreck sites. This particular wreck is of a ship that went down in the eighteen hundreds. After a few hundred years of weathering, the only discernable remains of the wreckage is a small pile of twisted metal where the anchor line is tied. Allegedly, this is the boiler of the vessel, and it's virtually indistinguishable from the rest of the ocean floor. A few large beams scatter about, but that's all there is to see. No matter—I'm here to catch dinner!

Approximately five minutes into the dive, I've gone about twenty yards from the flashing beacon at the tie-in point when I spy my first bug. He scuttles into a craggy hole under a pile of rocks. I sneak up to the where I see him go under. Unclipping a retractable pole from a rusty carabiner on my dive belt, I attempt to get behind the little bugger and coax him out of his hidey-hole. In just a few minutes, I have him out and into my catch bag.

Dinner! One down, one to go, and I'll be dining on lobster tonight . . . or so I thought. I can faintly make out the flashing beacon behind me when I set off down someone's wreck line in search of bug number two. I'm not more than dozen yards away when I spy something scuttling along the ocean floor. The bug instinctively escapes into another pile of rocks, and I work my way over to where I thought I saw him go under.

After spending a couple minutes searching around the rock pile, I see him stirring, his antenna revealing his hidden location. This one's not being so cooperative, and I find myself panting hard against my regulator. I breathe down valuable air, working to liberate my prize. It feels like ten minutes elapse before I finally get around to checking my air supply.

I vaguely make out the faintly glowing gauge in the darkness.

Fifteen hundred pounds.

Shit, I've already breathed down half my air! I must've been down here longer than I thought.

Looking around, I realize that I've drifted away from all the wreck lines. All I see around me are little piles of rubble in every direction. The surge picks up, and the current's moving more swiftly now. Visibility is down to three or four feet. I look around for the flashing beacon, but all I see are clouds of silt suspended all around me in a blanket of dense fog.

My heart's racing from exertion. The feeling of fear and dread are upon me. The rumble monster approaches. This is *not-good*. My heart pounds in my chest. I sense my limbic system go online and my ability to reason switch off as panic sets in. Panic is the number one cause of diver fatality, though coroner reports will often cite "heart failure resulting from breathing seawater." I intuitively know that somehow, I've got to reset my limbic system.

Diver training sets in. A practiced wreck diver conditions their subconscious to respond to panic with an intuitive survival instinct; this instinct launches an emergency reboot to bring the prefrontal cortex back online. I must stop exerting effort and breathe deeply to slow my heart rate. Grabbing onto a large boulder, I hang on as the surging current pulls my limp body to-and-fro, scraping and dragging me across the ocean floor. With each deep breath, my pulse slows, and I gradually regain composure. My prefrontal cortex comes back online, and rational decision-making returns. *Life comes down to choice, to cause and effect.* Cognitive reasoning tells me I have three options:

One: Continue the search for a wreck line or hope to find the flashing beacon.

Two: Begin a slow, free ascent to the surface, risking getting the bends or being whisked away, swept out to the open ocean.

Three: Use my lift bag to send up an emergency anchor line, creating safe passage to the surface.

I choose option *one.*

Releasing the boulder, I begin to drift. I'm hoping the current will return me somewhere within the vicinity of the anchor line, where I might spot the beacon or pass over somebody's line along the way. I float about twenty-five yards, then stop, grabbing another boulder to pause and recalibrate my approach.

Shit, no dice! I haven't seen any lines, and there's no flashing light in sight. All I can see in the cold, dark seawater is thick clouds of suspended silt. I check my air supply: *One thousand pounds!* I'd hit the rule of thirds: one-third of my air supply to head out, one-third to return to the anchor line, and one-third to return safely to the surface. I should be at the anchor line by now, making my ascent, and it's nowhere to be found.

Rumble, rumble, rumble. I again sense the approaching rumble monster. My limbic system fires up, and rational thinking goes back offline. I breathe harder and panic sets in.

Calm, calm, calm, repeats my subconscious. *Breathe, breathe, breathe,* responds my mind. *Everything's going to be okay.* My heart rate slows. *There's nothing to fear.* The rumble monster recedes. *You've got this.* It works! Reason then tells me three options remain:

One: Free ascent.

Two: Emergency anchor line.

Three: Do nothing and die.

I choose option *two*.

Steadying myself, I reach to retrieve the lift bag stowed in a pouch behind my air cylinder. Numb fingers in the icy water can't feel a thing through thick neoprene gloves. Fumbling, desperate minutes expire and breathing increases.

Screech! The rumble monster roars as fear and uncertainty returns with a fierce red passion. *You can't do this,* says the silent voice in my head. *You're gonna die here,* it continues, unrelenting. *I'm the answer to your prayers,* rages the rumble monster, and I recall my recent, desperate Prayer of Annihilation.

Breathing hard, instincts relaunch the emergency reboot protocol: *Calm, calm, calm,* repeats my subconscious. *Breathe, breathe, breathe,* replies my mind. *You're going to be okay.* Fear loosens its grip, and the rumble monster begins to recede again. *There's nothing to fear.* The rumblings of fear subside. *You've got this.* It works! Rational thought returns. I'm down to my final three options:

One: Free ascent.

Two: Keep working to free your lift bag and create an emergency anchor line.

Three: Who're you kidding? You're a goner.

I glance at my air supply: *five hundred pounds,* the divers' margin of error. It's the amount of air I should have at the dive's completion, having safely returned to the boat. Panic returns, limbic system takes over, heavy breathing.

This is it, this is the bottom—the *real* bottom. The Prayer of Annihilation I'd prayed the night before is being fulfilled. God's answering my prayer with imminent death, right on time, just as requested. Somehow it doesn't seem like such a great prayer anymore! My life flashes before my eyes. *There's so much more to live for. There's so much more left to do. I don't want to die anymore!*

This sucks, the voice returns. *Calm, calm, calm,* I say to myself. *Breathe, breathe, breathe.* It's doing no good. *It's going to be okay.* I know it's over. *There's nothing to fear.* I'm scared shitless. *You've got this*—but for the first time in my life, I really didn't. Prefrontal cortex shuts down, limbic system takes over, no choices remain.

I'd like to say I prayed at that moment, but I didn't. As my limbic system took over, there was no rational thought in that moment. So much for Ayn Rand's rational self-interest as a philosophy for life. I'd rationally managed to choose my way to a self-interested demise. There are limits to what I can do on my own steam. The "options":

One: You're gonna die.

Two: You're gonna die.

Three: God help me; I'm gonna fucking die!

Then I hear a different voice in my head. The diabolic one is replaced by an angelic whisper. *Dad?* asks a faint voice.

Dad, I love you, she quietly whispers.

Dad, I need you, growing eager, almost fearful, that voice of hope echoes in my head.

My angel, my precious daughter's voice is the last sensation I experience as I take my final dying breath. Everything fades to black as the world goes dark.

***

A timeless eternity goes by. I sense a Presence in the darkness. *To row, or not to row?* The Presence seeks an answer to the eternal question.

What's that? Something faintly shimmers in the dark. *Is that . . . a light?*

Glimmering through murky, clouding silt, I swim towards it. As I approach, I make out a shadowy shape. *Is that . . . a diver?* Emerging from the darkness, I glimpse the dim silhouette of a diver swimming against a faint flashing light. *The beacon! I see the flashing beacon!*

The blinking light signals the tie-in spot at the anchor, leading back to life. Thank God! I hadn't found it on my own, but in those final moments, God had *shown me the light*, literally.

A new faith is born in those final dark and dying moments—a revelation that rational self-interest, living a life relying on self-sufficiency, wouldn't be adequate to go on any further. I have purpose borne out by a higher power; I remember my daughter, love, and life!

I kick through the dark icy water and arrive at the flashing beacon marking the anchor line. I check my air supply: *One hundred pounds—shit!* I still have to get up the anchor line and spend a two-minute safety stop at twenty feet or I'll risk getting the bends, a dangerous condition in which bubbles of nitrogen are trapped in the body from ascending to the surface too quickly. My breathing's miraculously calm as I gradually make my way up the line. Again, I peer through the dark at the glowing pressure gauge: *Forty pounds.* My heart sinks. *I'm not going to make it.*

I experience an overwhelming sense of sadness for my daughter. The sea gradually turns to a lighter hue of gray. Sunlight penetrates the ocean surface above and the Carolina rig finally comes into view. The belly of the boat rests approximately twenty feet away. The pressure gauge reads *fifteen pounds.* There's no time for a safety stop, and I still have to navigate the suspended rope over to the submerged ladders! *I'll surely get the bends!* Gradually, I work my way hand-over-hand along the Carolina rig at twenty feet. I'm not sure how, but I'm somehow still pulling air through the regulator as time elapses.

One minute goes by. I pause at the rear of the boat; the submerged ladders are about fifteen feet above me. I take a final look at my gauge. It doesn't register at all; the needle rests against the stopper at zero. I take a final pull on the regulator, but there's no response! I'm completely out of air—nothing remains.

I hold my breath for as long as I can. With lungs burning, I'm at the verge of a blackout when I make a last-ditch effort and bolt for the surface. Drawing in a breath of seawater, my head crosses the threshold of the ocean surface. Gasping and sputtering, I spit out the spent regulator. Choking, I puke up saltwater into the freezing ocean waves. Miraculously, I breathe in a breath of air—my first breath living a new life!

Beep-beep-beep. Beep-beep-beep. My dive computer buzzes from my wrist. I look down, dreading to see the inevitable warning of an emergency ascent. I expect to see the little diver indicator with a cross though it, indicating that I've risen too quickly. Instead, I see the "finish okay" indicator flashing happily on the display. I realize the beeping is the sound of my dive computer indicating the safety-stop's been complete—*I've made it!*

Brought back from the dark depths of the abyss, I know my life's been spared to serve a greater purpose. I don't know what that purpose is yet, but I know it has nothing to do with the life I've been living. I've been living a life reliant upon the limiting beliefs of rational self-interest. I've been trusting in myself for everything, placing my faith in a God of personal responsibility. There's been no acknowledgement of altruism or the divine mystery of the numinous. I climb aboard and collapse onto the aluminum bench. I turn to see my dive buddy's beaming face, and he's grinning from ear to ear. Completely in the dark, he has no idea what just transpired.

"How was your dive, Al? Find anything *good* down there?" He motions to the catch bag at my side.

"Yeah, I did find something," I say, exhausted. "I think I've started to find an answer to the most important question in life," I pant.

"Oh, yeah? What question's that?" he asks.

"Who am I?" I respond.

"Hmmmm," he wonders, puzzled. "So, who are you?"

I pause, reflecting. "I can't say for sure," I reply, "but I'm certain of *one* thing."

"What's that?"

"*Who I am* isn't as important as how I've been living."

"Oh, yeah? And how've you been living?"

"I've been living it all for myself."

"So, what's different now?"

"I don't know. I just know that life's going to be very different now."

"Sounds like you're having an *identity crisis*!" he says, jokingly.

"Yeah, I'm definitely in need of a new identity." I pause to contemplate, knowing I'm very close to answering the mysterious question: *Who am I?*

Chapter 9:

Identity Crisis

An individual has not started living until he can rise above the narrow confines of his individualistic concerns to the broader concerns of all humanity.

—Martin Luther King, Jr.

January 2014: Philadelphia, Pennsylvania

"What's shakin', Al?" Vince asks with a smile. Vince is a founding partner at Legacy Advisors, LLC, a dear friend and coworker. His observation is accurate. The entire right side of my body's stiff, curled up tight, and shaking uncontrollably. The disease is progressing; my body's rapidly deteriorating. It's been seven years since the initial diagnosis, and I'm struggling with physical symptoms of the disease. Balance control, rigidity, and tremors: I see a future where an electric wheelchair might become a potential adaptation for my condition. I'm forty-one years old. I've enlisted a small army of medical professionals to combat the progressing symptoms that continue to march on:

Treatment Team
Primary-care physician
Neurologist
Neurosurgeon
Neuropsychiatrist
Occupational therapist
Physical therapist
Speech and language pathologist
Individual therapist

Collectively, we coordinate a treatment plan that includes near-daily visits to medical offices to manage the progressive symptoms of Parkinson's. While most recognizably a movement disorder, the most debilitating aspect of the disease is not visibly apparent. Substantial damage to my brain's executive center—which controls cognitive capabilities, like my working memory, and my ability to manage appointments, task lists, and agendas—impairs my ability to function reliably in my role as an investment manager. More than motor symptoms, these cognitive impairments acting in concert with a general deterioration of mood are the most debilitating set of symptoms I experience every day. Drugs, including levodopa and pramipexole, help to alleviate the motor complications and come with significant side effects, resulting in dramatic mood swings throughout the day and a worsening of manic episodes I experience regularly.

My medical team and I dance between finding treatment options to relieve my rapidly declining motor symptoms while minimizing side effects that impair cognition and mood. The dance venue's not a ballet; it seems more like a mosh pit! Pharmaceutical treatments come with the cost of drug-induced, manic episodes that've required my hospitalization.

Recreational drug and alcohol use is not advised. I'm now two-and-a-half years sober, working a twelve-step recovery program, and actively participating in intensive outpatient (IOP) group treatments. Earlier this morning, I attended a meeting of Alcoholics Anonymous where I met with my sponsor, Joe the Jeep. There's a close camaraderie in the Philadelphia recovery community. Regular attendees of *the rooms* (a place twelve-step meetings are held) are often given an anonymous handle. This maintains anonymity by not disclosing a person's actual last name. Joe's handle refers to the red jeep wrangler he drove when he sobered up. I'm known as "Shaky Al" because I shake from Parkinson's disease. It's an important distinction that explains that the reason I shake is not a result of delirium tremors, a symptom of early withdrawal from alcohol. It's also a term of endearment that says I'm "in the club."

I first interviewed at Legacy in 2010. I was afraid and shaking when I disclosed that I had Parkinson's disease, not knowing what their response would be. I feared I might have disqualified myself from the position I was interviewing for. We talked it through, and I explained there's no way to know how the symptoms might progress over the next five to ten years. The only thing I did know was that symptoms would progress significantly over that period.

My goal was to make it to fifty-five. I reasoned that by then I'd save enough money to retire early. I'd not anticipated the symptoms would progress this quickly. I find myself less than three years into my commitment to Legacy, no longer able to reliably function at my job. I feel guilty, like I've somehow misled them.

Legacy is an incredible organization, a true godsend. I've never worked for a group that's held so closely together as a corporate family. Having worked at the largest brokerage firm in the world, then experiencing both a startup and an established small business, I've learned that small business provides the best environment for those who find themselves working with a disability.

The commitment of the partners at Legacy has far outweighed the results they've gotten from my employment. I'm eternally grateful for their gracious attitude and willingness to take a risk on me. Legacy has worked very hard to prepare for my extended leave of absence. I'm about to undergo a risky procedure with promising results, but there's no guarantee I'll be able to return to work.

Researching the fast-approaching surgery has been like reading Mary Shelley's *Frankenstein*. I'll be awake as they drill two holes into my skull, penetrating deeply into my pre-frontal cortex. A pair of six-inch electrode-tipped leads will be placed into my subthalamic nucleus (STN). A magnetic charge will run along a set of cables, tunneled under my neck, and attached to a pair of pacemaker-like computer devices implanted in my chest.

Doctors inform me that there's a less-than-five-percent mortality rate, and that a young person has a very low risk associated with the procedure. The primary risk is infection; occurring in less than one percent of cases, this risk exists for any procedure where an external device is implanted into the body. I'm prepared for the worst, anticipating Tuesday morning's procedure with a freshly signed living will.

It's worth it—I'll risk almost anything for a fighting chance to relieve the perpetual shaking throughout my body. Additional benefits might include a fifty percent reduction in the drugs I take, which could extend my quality of life for many years. Most neurologists view the procedure as a last-case scenario, only to be considered after all other treatment options have been exhausted. The neurology group at Pennsylvania Hospital is more cutting-edge, taking a more progressive approach. They believe that individuals experiencing early-onset Parkinson's symptoms might benefit more in the long run by having risked the surgery early on. The promise of an improved quality of life and a reduction in pharmaceutical symptom control balances the risks of the procedure.

As a professional risk manager, I've learned how to take calculated risks. Harkening back to the rumble monster, risk management has been a winning formula I've successfully used to navigate life's path.

Legacy's clients are privately-owned business owners. Many of those clients understood the risks they were in their businesses and were seeking to construct investment portfolios minimizing risk. Others were more willing to accept volatility for increased returns, all of our portfolios were structured consider all facets of their planning objectives. The firm never did anything in a vacuum. The approach was holistic 100% of the time. However, all of our clients wanted and needed to understand risk. Working with hedge funds since the mid-nineties, I'm an expert in evaluating risk and implementing solutions that minimize loss while capturing positive returns.

In all the years I've spent working with individuals and their investments, I've discovered that nearly everyone has the same goal when hiring someone else to manage their wealth: *Make as much money as you can without losing it!* Legacy's president is concluding the last annual meeting I'd attend when I raise my hand. "Do you mind if I say something to the group?" I ask.

"Uhhh, sure Alex, go ahead," he nervously replies.

I stand up and walk to the front of the conference room. There are about thirty employees present, each of whom I'd come to know personally since working at the firm. I feel a knot form in my throat, and strong emotions well up as I begin to speak. "I was driving to the office this morning thinking about what I'd say to you all today. What I was thinking about was all the things that *they* say. *They* say a lot of things, don't they?"

The room chuckles.

"*They* say things like, 'When you're on your deathbed, and the lights are about to go out, you take in your last breath, and what's going through your head is never *I should have worked harder.*'

"*They* say that no one's epitaph will ever read: '*Should've spent more time at the office.*'"

I look out to a room full of heads nodding yes.

"*They* say that it's the time you spend with your family that matters most. Yet, here we all find ourselves, sacrificing time away from family to further the cause of Legacy and our clients."

More head nods as the president shifts uncomfortably in his chair.

"I can tell you that on Tuesday morning, when the gurney rolls into the operating room, and the lights are about to go out, I already know what I'm going to be thinking as I take my last breath. What *they* don't say is what's really going through your head at that time."

The room is silent.

"The questions that are actually running around in your head are . . ."

You could hear a pin drop as I struggle to hold back tears.

"Did I make a difference? Did I do enough? Did I impact the world and live my life in a way that honors the difference I tried to make? These are the real questions we ask when we have everything to lose."

I look out at the people in the room. I see that each one has walked this journey with me for the last three years. They've tolerated the mistakes, and they've celebrated the small victories we've had along the way.

"So, on my way to work, I found myself asking, did we do enough for this company, for our clients? Unfortunately, I know the answer is no—we did not do enough, but we tried our best." My voice cracks as tears well up. "When I first came to Legacy and interviewed with the partners, I told them I had this disease. I said I didn't know if I'd have five years or ten years left to commit. They took a risk and hired me. They took a chance on me, and their gamble didn't pay." It's difficult to speak, but I press on, addressing the newly hired people. "You're working for the most extraordinary group of people I've ever met. The corporate body of Legacy works together in a way that I've not experienced anywhere else. So, when you go home today, just remember that you're working for a company that truly impacts this community. This company changes lives. I'll know when I close my eyes and breathe what could be my last breath on Tuesday that we've done the best we can—and that's enough for me."

I conclude by thanking the president and partners at Legacy before returning to my seat. I've spoken my peace, thanking those who've gone beyond their call of duty to help me in my most valiant fight. I'm truly grateful. I have no idea where I'd be today if it weren't for the difference these dedicated individuals have made in my life. I'll forever owe a debt of gratitude to my corporate family at Legacy. I owe them my life. Thank you, each one of you. You know who you are.

Doctor God: Part Three

Tuesday comes more quickly than I want it to. It's a typical, dreary gray morning, and my neurosurgeon, Doctor God, arrives on the scene. Dressed in a fashionable trench coat, his compassionate bedside manner arrives with him. Doctor God is a total rock star. He's the most credentialed doctor that's ever cared for me, with an undergraduate degree from Harvard, a master's degree from Stanford, a doctorate in medicine from McGill University, and a further post-graduate degree from the Wharton School of Business. In addition to impeccable academic credentials, Doctor God has performed more deep brain stimulation (DBS) procedures than anyone else on the planet. He's been performing the procedure for over fifteen years, including several years as an experimental researcher at Pennsylvania University, before DBS received official FDA approval in 1998.

"Ready to go, kid?" He smiles as I roll into the operating room. Beaming lights illuminate the room like angelic sunrays descending from heaven as the heavy sedation keeps me halfway between reality and dreamland. The initial half of the procedure is performed while I'm awake. It's a truly horrific thought knowing Doctor Frankenstein is prodding my open brain with pulsating electrodes, looking for the right responses, all while I'm awake. Surprisingly, the powerful sedation quells my fear entirely, making the procedure nearly pleasurable!

"Tap your thumb to your pointer finger," I recall him saying to me in my tranced-out state. I remember peering through the head-gear contraption that held my head in place at my shaky right hand. No longer shaking, my now-steady hand performs flawlessly—an experience worth being awake for! The operating room staff erupts in applause as the lights go dark and I enter the second phase of the surgery.

"This is going to feel like drinking a six-pack of beer in under five minutes," I remember the young anesthesiologist saying before I reenter the eternal dark. Cables are tunneled under my scalp and down my neck on either side where they're attached to a pair of pacemaker-like neurogenerators in my chest.

***

Beep, beep, beep. The intensive care unit's electrocardiogram sounds off rhythmically.

"How're you doing?" I hear the comforting voice of my father before falling back into darkness, unable to answer.

Light floods the room and I awaken to the scent of rubbing alcohol. My father and mother are sitting on a hard-cushioned sofa in the sanitized hospital room. I look down at my calm right arm. I'm not shaking at all—the procedure worked!

"It's going to be okay," says the soothing voice of my mother, her soft caressing touch on my forehead.

"You're going to be just fine," I hear my father say, his voice confident, reassuring, and comforting.

New paths of possibility emerge as my life's course is altered once again. I'd no longer experience the continuous shaking of my right hand. Motor symptoms abate. The promise of reduced dependency on pharmaceutical treatments by as much as fifty percent becomes a reality.

In fact, this promise is far exceeded.

"You don't have to take any levodopa now, if you don't want to," beams Doctor God during a follow-up appointment.

I graciously accept the suggestion. Levodopa, which involves a four-times-daily drug regimen, comes with severe side effects. I titrate down, and the oscillating mood swings I had experienced gradually begin to even out, and then they disappear entirely. A one-hundred-percent reduction in pharmaceutical intervention is achieved: a nearly unheard-of result, even for Doctor God.

***

Six months into my recovery, I experience another nearly unheard-of statistic.

I've been dogged by an excruciating migraine headache all week. While driving to a physical therapy appointment one day, I find myself using every ounce of concentration just to keep the car in the lane. When I finally arrive at the appointment, the physical therapist takes one look at me and says, "You're going to the emergency room right now!"

Thirty minutes later, I'm back in the operating room with Doctor God. Recovering in the intensive care unit, he greets me with a sullen expression. "You had a massive abscess. You're lucky to be alive." I learn that I'm one of the unlucky few who have experienced the lottery-winning-odds of contracting an infection from the implanted device.

"A few months of intravenous antibiotics should do it," cheered the infectious disease expert in his not-Doctor-God bedside manner. Switching out an IV bag full of fluid four times a day, I'm fed a constant drip through a PICC-line (peripherally inserted central catheter) stuck in my arm. I'm laid up in my Philadelphia apartment for several months before the infection finally clears. It becomes increasingly clear that the fate of my career is sealed.

Three more months pass, and I've depleted all my savings. Surgical complications have left me with hospital bills and neurological impairments that severely handicap my cognitive abilities. Unable to reliably perform at Legacy, I'm faced with the prospect permanent disability. I'm deathly afraid of losing the capacity to earn a living. Ominous clouds roll in, casting a shadow on an uncertain future. I'm overcome with a sense of hopelessness, grief, and desperation. *I have a daughter and ex-wife—how will I provide for them?* I wonder. I undergo endless visits to neurologists with no end in sight, perpetual physical therapy, and expensive pharmaceutical treatments. There's a sinking sensation of dread in the pit of my stomach. My head swims with doubt and uncertainty—all questions and no answers.

I meet with Legacy's human resources director who assures me I have options, as well as some tough decisions to make.

"Legacy's long-term-disability policy will pay sixty percent of your annual income," says the benefit plan representative over a conference room speakerphone.

"Sixty percent? For how long?" I ask.

"Until you retire—that's age sixty-seven for you. Legacy's insured you with the best possible coverage."

I breathe out a huge sigh of relief; the disability plan will provide a sustainable-enough income that I'll be able to take care of myself and my family.

"Here's the tough decision," responds the human resources director. "Are you prepared to hang it up?"

Pausing, I contemplate what it means to give up my life's work. I've invested over twenty years building my career. My work is nearly indistinguishable from who I am. It's been my identity for so long—who will I be if I'm not my work? I'd persevered through decades of gyrating economic calamities, and I'd spent countless hours sacrificing family time. It had all exacted a toll on my health and wellbeing—but I've been well rewarded for my effort.

It doesn't feel I have much choice in the matter. I'm left with an empty feeling, like I'm being benched from the team. Sadly, the impaired cognitive functioning leaves few prospects for remaining in my line of work. I pull the ripcord. *This must be my golden parachute,* I reason. Somehow, it wasn't what I'd expected it would be, but at least I'd be retiring with dignity.

***

Months later, I find myself back in the rooms of Alcoholics Anonymous performing service work. I visit prisoners in halfway houses struggling with addiction. I host meetings in church basements. I make coffee and straighten chairs. Service work is a pillar of the recovery community, and it feels good to help others. I also miss the energy and excitement of taking risks while managing vast fortunes of other people's money.

"Shaky Al, is that you? I hardly recognized you walking in—I can't believe what I'm seeing!" My sponsor, Joe Jeep, was in shock.

This is the first he's seen of the *new me*. I've been away from the rooms for over six months, laid up in my apartment, recovering from surgery and other complications. I'm not shaking at all. I'm no longer hunched over in a twisted knot with my arm curled against my chest, shuffling along awkwardly like an old man. This was the condition he'd last seen me in, and the comparison is shocking.

"Well, Joe, I learned to walk again. I can't trade stocks anymore, but it's definitely still me!" I cheer. By this point, I have realized how much time is required to treat the symptoms of Parkinson's; it's a full-time job, when done properly. What I didn't realize until I stopped working was how much stress exacerbates disease symptoms.

"What're you going to do with yourself now that you're retired, Al?" "I don't know, I think I'll take that art class I always wanted to."

Joe's a retired Philadelphia School District art teacher.

"Wow, that's not gonna last long. You'd better keep me on speed dial," he says with a grin. Joe knows my drive for "more" better than anyone; an art class isn't enough to keep me occupied and out of trouble.

"You're not thinking you'll be the retired businessman who lolls in the Florida sunshine in the winter, complaining of the sad state of the nation, are you?" he says, referencing a passage from the Big Book of Alcoholics Anonymous.

"Nah," I reply, "I know better than that! People don't ever retire, Joe—we just move on to doing different things. One thing's *for certain*, Joe."

"Oh yeah? This ought to be good. Name one thing that you know *for certain*."

"I'm gonna change the world!" I laugh.

"Yeah, you're gonna change the world all right. Just let me know when so I can get out of the way," he chuckles. Then he adds, "You know, there's one thing I know *for certain*."

"Yeah, what's that, Joe?"

"Shaky Al's gonna need a new identity—you're not shakin' anymore!"

"You're probably right, Joe. But I just can't seem to shake this nagging question I've always had."

"What's that?"

"*Who am I?*"

Joe always has the same response to my endless philosophizing. "Oh brother, Shaky, try and keep it simple, stupid. Do me a favor, okay?"

"Sure, Joe."

"Never forget that who you are is a grateful recovering alcoholic. Your primary purpose is to stay sober and help another alcoholic achieve sobriety. Working with others, being of service—that's who you are. Got it?"

"Yeah, I got it Joe."

"I'm not sure you do, Al. Alcoholics Anonymous is a simple program for complicated people. Just don't drink and get your ass to a meeting, okay?""Sure thing, Joe—I got it!" *Who am I, really? Am I really an alcoholic?* Wonders the lion at the door called denial.

PART THREE: ASCENSION

Chapter 10:

Blue Rover

Whatever the mind of man can conceive and believe, it can achieve.

—Napoleon Hill

November 2016: Austin, Texas

"It's a La-Z-Boy on wheels," says the shopkeeper at Easy Street Recumbents. "Have a seat." He gently pats the soft padding of the bucket seat of a brand-new three-wheel recumbent trike. Glistening with a glossy-blue paint job, the name "Rover" is emblazoned on its side. *"Blue Rover," a fitting name, I muse.*

It's been just over two years since my fateful brain surgery. Rare complications with the implanted stimulators have left me with permanent brain damage. The damage extends into my cerebellum and occipital lobe, impairing balance and spatial recognition. While many symptoms have abated during recovery, those that remain challenge my ability to ride a two-wheeled bike. The suggested adaptation: a three-wheeled, recumbent-design trike with a large bucket seat. I can't help but think the "La-Z-Boy on wheels" is an unwelcome compromise.

Manufactured by TerraTrike, the shining blue Rover's recumbent design provides increased stability and forgiveness to accommodate for my lack of balance. "The Rover model can be customized with larger wheels and mountain treads for off-road trekking," says the shopkeeper.

Sadly, the transition from a two-wheeled mountain bike to a three-wheeled trike comes at a cost. Single-track mountain biking trails would prove inaccessible. If I were to go off-road, I'd be limited to wide logging roads and jeep trails able to accommodate the wider wheelbase.

A necessary compromise, I reason, pondering the regrettable circumstances that have left me unable to ride the more exhilarating trails that are the hallmark of adventurous mountain biking. With staunch determination, I reach over the bike's handlebars to steady myself. Straddling the cumbersome aluminum frame, a rush of endorphins surge through me—a reminder of the flow-state I'd experienced during long rides. Euphoria promptly evaporates, replaced by resignation. Subconsciously, my body resists. Stiff muscles tighten, groaning against the persistent symptoms of physical limitations. The adaptation feels forced, leaving me with uncomfortable feelings of resentment.

"Okay, let's give this a shot!" I say, half-resigned, as I muster the courage to set out in a new direction in life. I plop down into the cushiony bucket seat. "You're right—this thing feels way better than a conventional bike seat!" Immediately, my lower back relaxes. Stiff, cramped muscles soften. A sense of ease and comfort cascades over me. The warm, glowing sensation of sipping a smooth, twenty-year-old scotch comes to mind. I let out a long sigh. Contrasted against the hunched position forced by a two-wheel bike, the trike's recumbent design is extremely comfortable.

"It *is* like sitting in a La-Z-Boy on wheels!" I echo the shopkeeper's cheerful sentiment before pushing off towards the parking lot for a test drive.

My right thumb clicks the shift lever. Legs press hard against protesting pedals that resist the difficult crankshafts. The rear derailleur awkwardly sputters into place. Grinding and popping sounds emerge from the rear sprocket as the chain searches for traction before finding a firm resting place. The rear cassette engages. Awkwardly, the bike lurches. "Coming through, coming through!" I announce boldly, gliding effortlessly through the store. Soft tires cushion its rigid frame as it clatters down an aluminum ramp onto the parking lot pavement with a bang.

Suddenly, a distant memory interrupts the comfortable moment. In my mind's eye, I flashback to 1992, where I find myself at the Winter Park ski resort in Colorado.

***

I'm twenty years old, training to be an adaptive ski instructor at the National Sports Center for the Disabled (NCSD), the largest adaptive ski program in the nation.

"Coming through, coming through!" barks a six-foot-tall NSCD volunteer. His strong upper body heaves a mass of plexiglass and aluminum hardware connecting a bucket seat to a shock absorber mounted to a pair of short, wide skis. The device is called a sit-ski, an accommodation for those limited by a variety of disabling conditions. It enables the disabled person to glide effortlessly down wide mountains slopes. I'm sitting in the bucket seat of the sit-ski as a part of a group experiment. We're each taking turns experiencing what it's like to be a participant in our program—that is, a person with a disability in a sit-ski.

The scent of coconut sunscreen hangs in the cold, dry rocky mountain air, merging with the distinctive buttery taste of Carmex lip balm on my parched lips. A bulging crowd of skiers impatiently shifts around as they await their turn to ride lift number five; they are weekend warriors, anxious to get to the top of the mountain.

"Make way, people!" shouts the instructor in a hoarse voice with a twinge of annoyance. Impatient skiers awkwardly shuffle aside, clearing a path for us to make our way through the crowd. The sound of skis and poles clack together, interrupting the otherwise orderly line of skiers. We approach the icy loading platform where a pair of energetic lift operators slow down the chairlift to accommodate my special needs. Tears well up in my eyes. For the first time,

I experience what it feels like to be "special" and in need of help. I don't like the feeling. I don't want help—a not-so-subtle acknowledgement that I'm different. In that moment, the only thing I want is to be like everyone else. I feel disenfranchised and spiteful.

Taking aim, I angrily shoot back at the eager lift operators, insisting, "I've got this!" Ignoring my frustration, they dutifully assist in loading the cumbersome sit-ski onto the slowly approaching chair.

Back at the lodge, the training group shares how it felt to be sitting in the bucket seat of the sit-ski. "I don't want to be perceived as having *special needs*," says one participant. The group nods and murmurs in agreement. "I felt their pity. I reacted with a sense of disdain for those offering help. They look at me with inauthentic gratitude—they're grateful that they're not like me."

"It felt shameful. I was put on the defensive," says yet another.

The consensus is a feeling of shame, disappointment, and anger towards those treating us differently, despite their helpful intentions.

Ultimately, the sit-ski exercise provided us with unique access to feelings of compassion—a profound empathy for the human condition, and a window into how our participants might feel about their disability. While other people are helpful and accommodating towards us with special needs, the experience of being "special" isn't special at all. It's the experience of being different. It's humbling.

***

Startled by a jarring thump, the memory ends in a flash. One moment I'm in the sit-ski, and the next I find myself back at the bike shop sitting in the bucket seat of the Blue Rover. Reminiscent of the sit-ski experience from nearly thirty years ago, feelings of shame, resentment, and anger return. I recognize my anger as a smoke screen for fear. I sit with my feelings and observe them, acknowledge them. I fear I'll never ride a two-wheeled mountain bike again. I fear my life of adventure will be replaced by dull complacency. My anger turns to grief and resignation. A knot forms in my throat as I attempt to hold back tears. It's no use, and I begin to weep.

Why do I grieve a future that hasn't happened yet? I wonder.

"Hey, man, are you okay?" asks the shopkeeper.

I mentally check out, drifting off into deep thoughts regarding my circumstances. I'm reminded of the moment I was diagnosed; I was thirty-five when it happened. The hopes and dreams I'd held for the future were smashed. My entire life was before me, and the diagnosis had felt like a prison sentence. I recall that fateful day, remembering my hopeful dreams. *Someday, maybe in a faraway distant future, I'll finally find peace of mind,* I had thought back then. In my someday-maybe fantasy future, I'd be free of worry and discontent. *Someday, I'll find myself aging gracefully with the one I'll grow old with. Someday, I'll be sitting on the front porch of a beautiful house with my beloved. We'll sit in a pair of rocking chairs, holding hands, smiling as the sun sets over a backdrop of a beautiful mountain golf course.*

This hopeful, someday-maybe future was shattered. I'm struck by the reality that I'm on a new path, one that must be acknowledged.

***

The Oxford English Dictionary defines pathology simply as, "The science of the causes and effects of diseases." In essence, we study the paths by which disease comes. There are limits to medical science. There have been no specific causal pathogens linked to Parkinson's disease. Without knowing a direct cause for the disease, identifying a cure is problematic. What's known is that something happens to our brain cells that effects their ability to generate dopamine-producing neurons. The primary suspect is a genetic predisposition, combined with exposure to yet-unidentified environmental toxins. Through genetic mapping, science has succeeded in identifying specific genes that point to Parkinson's disease. The nature of what causes these genes to mutate remains a mystery. We're left to forge our way through a tangled web of symptoms, treating them individually as they march on.

Originally described as the "shaking palsy" in 1817, the symptoms of Parkinson's disease have been observed for hundreds of years. I'd experienced the chronic progression of these symptoms over the ten-year period following my initial diagnosis. The observable impact includes tremors, difficulty walking, a hunched back with stiff slowness, and painful tightness. The cause: an eighty percent reduction in dopamine-producing neurons.

I'm told the rate of progression and types of symptoms from Parkinson's are unique to each person. While our symptoms are variable, and the pace of onset uncertain, our ultimate prognosis is known with certainty. It's not pretty. Individuals with late-stage Parkinson's disease face difficulties with bathing and dressing themselves. We live with debilitating stiffness, constant tremors, and significant pain. Other symptoms severely limit independent living, forcing reliance on a team of care providers. While not terminal, complications arising from the disease often are. The primary cause of death for those with Parkinson's disease is pneumonia, often resulting from hospitalization due to fall risk or difficulties swallowing.

Early in my diagnosis, I found hope in denial. The emergence of early-stage symptoms doesn't always mean a person has Parkinson's, and misdiagnosis isn't uncommon. Complicating matters further, there aren't any objective tests that point to a definitive diagnosis. General physicians are often the first to point out the possibility, and even after seeking an experienced neurologist, there's still a chance of misdiagnosis. I'd been evaluated by two respected and highly qualified neurologists, yet my denial lasted nearly five years. It was easier to deny Parkinson's than accept the reality of my progressing symptoms. The effort required to live in that denial was tortuous. Eventually, symptoms progressed to a point where the condition became medically undeniable. For me, giving up denial meant giving up the hope that I'd somehow been misdiagnosed. While counter-intuitive, the experience of giving up this hope was immensely liberating. It's curious how this perspective seemed to anger others—particularly those with best intentions to offer hope and support.

The delusion that I was like others who didn't have Parkinson's had to be smashed. Many people recovering from a variety of ailments will testify that there's true freedom in finding the courage to leave hopeless denial behind. Denial doesn't serve us—it's devoid of hope. Experience shows that admitting we have a condition, like alcoholism, is an essential first step in recovery; admitting that I had Parkinson's was no different. I saw that truth is seeing the world as it is—not as I wanted it to be, or how I thought it should be. It's been said that the truth will piss you off before it sets you free. I had to walk through the anger of denial, facing it head-on, before I could be liberated from its prison. I recognized that I wasn't defined by my circumstances. A burden lifted and new hope was born when I accepted completely that I had Parkinson's.

Next, I embarked upon another hopeful path. I was met by an impassioned group of individuals claiming to have found the elusive miracle cure. With near-religious fanaticism, they persisted in a belief that modern medicine simply focuses in the wrong place. Their belief was fueled by a theory that greedy corporations conspire to create dependency on the drugs they sell. Specialized diets, homeopathic or herbal remedies, spiritual healing practices, or any myriad of alternative healing methods are where a ready cure might be discovered. Some of the more common alternative cures that medical science avoids include: essential oil therapies, CBD oil, marijuana, and natural vitamin supplements. The list of suggested remedies is endless, and there's usually a "something-to-them" curiosity that appeals to our senses. Caution is warranted to any of these approaches—there's a gullible aspect to hope that has us entertain all kinds of notions.

Blind recommendations are made, and strong opinions are expressed with an insistent fervor. There are heartfelt testimonials claiming cures from all kinds of ailments. "You should try this" is followed by "I know someone who swears by it!" These claims usually come from people who don't have Parkinson's, but they have experience treating some of the symptoms. Some people directly profit from selling the "cure-all." Not all claims are fraudulent, but history is littered with a storied past of snake-oil sales that seems to repeat in every generation. While their motives are mostly well intended, people don't realize their desire to be helpful leaves me with the message that I'm not doing enough, or my efforts are somehow insufficient.

I prefer the term "complementary medicine" to "alternative medicine," and I'm cautious to dismiss all of these approaches outright. I'd be foolish to fully discount the many examples pointing to improvements and the testimonials of so many who have benefited from such approaches. I'm an advocate for wellness practices, mainly those which serve to improve virtually anyone's quality of life at any stage. We are all well advised to embrace healthy lifestyle choices. Over the years I've complemented my treatment plan with a ketogenic diet, select vitamins and nutritional supplements, regular exercise, acupuncture, massage, qigong, dancing, and mosaic art, just to name a few. Alternative approaches are part of a comprehensive, holistic treatment plan that works for me. I share what's working and avoid giving unsolicited advice. I'm careful to acknowledge that what does work for me might not work for someone else. When discussing alternative medicine, my top-ten list of common-sense considerations that universally apply include:

ALTERNATIVE-MEDICINE CONSIDERATIONS

Be Informed: Do your research but know the limits of your own medical expertise.

Internet Accuracy: The internet is a treasure trove of unverified data—don't confuse information with advice.

Unregulated: Non-FDA-approved remedies may produce harmful interactions, communicate with your doctor.

Guru's: Caution's warranted when considering miracle cures promised by the "experts" of alternative practices.

Third-Party Testimony: Be aware when a friend-of-a-friend's experience is offered as the primary source of evidence for a remedy's effectiveness.

Trust Me: Products promoted with sentiments of: "Trust me, it works" usually require additional due diligence.

Caveat Emptor: Buyer beware—While many have good intentions, beware of hucksters working a side-hustle!

Hard Sales Tactics: Look out for pushy salespeople creating a "must-act-now" sense of urgency in their pitch.

Multi-Level Marketing: "Income-opportunities" offering promising results for redistributors may not work out.

Facts & Opinions: Advice is an opinion, usually backed up by facts. Learn to distinguish the facts from the opinions.

The list of alternative healing modalities is endless, and their pursuit can be exhausting. Though I believe in miracles, I reserve a healthy skepticism towards those claiming to have discovered the miracle cure. Whether conventional or alternative, I acknowledge and honor the unique path each person takes in treating their symptoms. When I stopped looking at claims that someone had discovered the miracle cure, it freed me to start living my life again. Today I love my life for all it is and for all it isn't, exactly as it is and exactly as it isn't—that's true freedom!

I've not abandoned hope for an *actual* cure. I'm confident that research efforts will one day identify exactly what causes brain cells to stop producing dopamine and how to regenerate the capacity to do so. I remain hopeful that a cure will be discovered someday—maybe even within my lifetime! With a ten-year-plus FDA-approval window for new treatments, I'm not holding my breath. As research efforts are tirelessly pursued, I'm committed to living life to the fullest, in each moment. I'm grateful for the contribution of our collective efforts. I'm touched, moved, and inspired by those wanting to make a difference. I believe in the promise of the Michael J. Fox Foundation for all of us:

> **OUR PROMISE:** The Michael J. Fox Foundation is dedicated to finding a cure for Parkinson's disease through an aggressively funded research agenda and to ensuring the development of improved therapies for those living with Parkinson's today.

With best intentions, people continue to encourage me to never give up. *You can fight this!* they say. Western culture has a rich history of warfare and winning. This attitude affords little space for compassion or empathy for what we're fighting. Those facing incurable disease are vehemently encouraged to resist, to fight, and to somehow overcome something that presently has no cure. It's "un-American" to admit defeat, and it's "unacceptable" for a person with a chronic illness not to resist and put up a fight.

This sentiment of "don't give up" is particularly strong from those who provide support for loved ones with chronic illness. It stems from a basic human experience: it's uncomfortable to be in the presence of someone in pain when there's nothing we can do to stop it. Lacking power to alter the course of a prognosis, it's easier to encourage someone to fight than it is to sit with them and accept they're in pain. There's always the suggestion of uninvited advice, something more to do, something else to try, another treatment to pursue. We lose sight of our humanity when we become intolerant to anothers pain.

I gave up the idea there was something more I had to do in order to be cured; that's when I found true peace of mind and became available for others in a way that most people can't. This awareness is where empathy and compassion begin, and it's sorely missing in our culture of resistance and fighting.

Unlike cancer, a person doesn't beat Parkinson's into remission. It's not a disease that's presently overcome, and I'm not a survivor. That's not to say I don't engage the battle in my own way. I pick my battles and fight the good fight where it serves me. I acknowledge there's always going to be *something-more* that I can do. I've discovered that *something-more* exacts a toll on the psyche. *Something-more* is endless and exhausting. *Something-more* is unnecessary. What's missing in our culture is the capacity to be at peace with what-is instead of our never-ending pursuits in search of *something-more* to do.

A challenge that's greater than resisting or fighting is cultivating the ability to be with pain and acknowledge the presence of limitations. I don't overcome limits, I move through them, not around them. By acknowledging my limitations, I get unstuck from the bog of denial—that quagmire formed out of endless resistance and fighting. Paradoxically, it's inside of the acknowledgment of my limitations where I find the possibility of a *World Without Limit.*

It's a rare individual who can sit with discomfort long enough to distinguish their limitations from their discomfort. I've been blessed with a front-row seat!

A question emerges: *What do I do after all the cards have been dealt, the game is at its end, and I'm left holding an unplayable hand?*

The game of life is like that; seemingly impossible moments befall each of us at some point or another. I find myself amidst the effects of life's circumstances—a place where there seems no path to possibility. These perceived limits lead to a crossroads, a binary option: fold or bluff. Neither seems very inspiring. Folding isn't an option for most of us, so we bluff. Wisdom comes when we realize that we're all bluffing: at being certain, at being prepared for what comes next, at being immortal.

The game of life isn't always about winning; more often, it's about bluffing. A more meaningful question to ask is this: *What am I willing to risk to stay in the game?* I played my winning hand long ago. Bluffing has enabled me to stay in the game longer. When I gave up the necessity of winning, I discovered the power of surrender. The winners of the world despise this logic, but in fact, surrender doesn't mean giving up, it means moving to the winning side! With nothing to lose, I'm liberated to make new choices from a different point of view. "Nothing-to-lose" grants us the freedom to risk everything, and new paths of possibility emerge. I discovered that in the game of life, I could be all-in with an unplayable hand!

"You okay?" repeats the shopkeeper with genuine concern.

Being present to grief, a force greater than that which caused it in the first place, sparks inspiration. From nothing-to-lose, a new possibility is born. Glimpsing a future that's somehow already happened, I experience *jamais vu:* the sense of something familiar being encountered for the first time. The fabric of space and time tears open, and a vision emerges into existence. From the depths of the Pacific Ocean floor in Hawaii, I'm ascending thirty-five thousand feet to the summit of the Mauna Kea volcano. Halfway up the ascent, I reach the shoreline, where I pause for a moment to reflect. The rear tire of a bike sinks into warm, soft, sand. Cool ocean waves lap against the wheel. Clear blue water splashes onto the frame. In my vision, I set off again, ascending ever higher, until I reach the volcano's summit. I reach an elevation so high that I can see clouds thousands of feet beneath me. The Gemini Observatory comes into view.

The vision is exhilarating. It powerfully replaces a dismal view of my future with a vision that seems unattainable, yet somehow, I've already realized it! *You've got this*, confidently speaks an inner voice.

"You know, I'm gonna ride this thing up the side of a volcano!" I enthusiastically exclaim to the shopkeeper.

"Hey, man, whatever gets you going." He grins, sensing an imminent transaction. The experience in the bike shop completes a circle in my life. The story of resignation I'd been telling myself disappears, dissolving into love and compassion. With a deep sense of empathy for all those who have special needs, I've received a gift from a higher power that allows me to connect to others who share this experience. I'm imbued with gratitude. Nothing is left; I'm complete.

"I'll take it," I exclaim.

"You won't be disappointed," the shopkeeper beams enthusiastically in response.

Who am I? wonders a subconscious voice.

"I'm all in, with nothing to Lose" IT responds confidently.

Chapter 11:
World Without Limit

Freedom comes from understanding the limits of our own power, and the natural limits set in place by divine providence. By accepting life's limits and inevitabilities, and working with them rather than fighting them, we become free.

—*Epictetus, 341 BC*

July 2017: Austin, Texas, 5:00 a.m.

It's early in the morning on a Tuesday at the Austin airport. Workers mull about the baggage area in a zombie-like trance. I'm greeted by a cheery smiling woman with a nametag that reads "Joy." She radiates with a caffeinated, buzzy glow. *Nobody should be at work this early!* Joy's overly enthusiastic demeanor annoys me right from the get-go.

Clickety-clickety-clickety—she taps the keyboard in a manner that only airline ticketing-agents can. "That'll be four hundred dollars," beams Joy from behind the American Airlines ticket counter. "Each way," she adds after a short pause, punctuating her remark with a gleaming smile. I'd be flying to Hawaii in less than forty-eight hours. I'm struggling to comprehend the expense of transporting the oversized bike, which far exceeds American Airlines' domestic baggage requirements.

"That's eight hundred dollars, round trip!" I exclaim in disbelief. "That's nearly the cost of my ticket!" I stammer, not comprehending how this could be possible. "I was told that transporting the bike container wouldn't be an issue—they said the bike's considered sporting equipment, like skis or a golf bag."

Joy shakes her head, dutifully reciting the airline's policy. "One carry-on and one personal item is allowed, free of charge. Checked bags are twenty-five dollars each, and additional restrictions apply. Checked bags cannot exceed 62 linear inches, calculated by total length, width, and height. Further additional charges apply for bags exceeding fifty pounds." She again punctuates her disclosure with that annoying, gleaming smile. I'm less than inspired.

"What is it exactly that you have in there?" Joy quizzically gestures at the giant case resting on the scale.

"It's a three-wheeled recumbent bike." I briefly explain my circumstances.

"You might want to check with TSA security," she suggests. "It's possible they'd consider that thing a mobility device, but that'd be up to them."

"You mean like a wheelchair?" I stutter.

"A *mobility device*," she emphasizes curtly with a smug, politically correct tone.

I'm insulted, and defiant. The beastly, rugged off-road bike that I've invested months training on couldn't possibly be considered a wheelchair! I'd just returned from thirty days of training at high-altitude in Colorado to prepare for this trial of magnificent endurance. Joy clearly doesn't have any appreciation that I've just conquered the treacherous logging roads of Cordova Pass!

"Okay, I'll sort it out somehow." I storm off. I recognize my anger as fear. The rumble monster screeches, raging from within. All my instincts tell me to run away. I'm afraid. I pause to get present to my fears. *What am I really afraid of?* I peer into my mind's eye, and the vision begins to blur. The sound of ocean waves lapping up against the Blue Rover fades into silence. The sensation of warm sand between my toes begins to dull. The vision of the windy summit of Mauna Kea, with its observatories peering into an infinite universe, is now clouded by doubt.

The volcano rumbles. *I'm afraid I'm not gonna make it, that I'm not enough, that I'm insufficient.* Fear is an illusion, but it seems so real in this moment. What does it mean to know fear? How do I pass through the darkness of doubt, cross the threshold of fear, and step into the sunlight of certainty? It starts with an awareness of my limitations. But what does it mean to know my limits?

Know: To be aware of the truth or factuality of something.
Limit: Something that bounds, constrains, or confines.

The dimensions of the bike transport exceed the carrier's baggage allowance. It's not permitted to travel under the plane with me to Hawaii. The truth: The airline's policy is what it is—not as I hope it to be or think it should be.

I'm stuck. *What limit am I'm backed up against?* I pause to assess the circumstances. A quick google search of the American Airlines baggage policy confirms that Joy's assessment is correct. The policy clearly states that checked bags cannot exceed 62 linear inches, calculated by total length, width, and height. Regardless of any effort on my part, the limit set by the carrier is what it is—that's not about to change. Inside of the limit itself is where I'd look to discover a new possibility. *There must be an adaptation that would empower me to work through the limit without trying to step over it.*

I browse Amazon.com, searching for the largest traveling bag that can be delivered via Amazon Prime within twenty-four-hours. I calculate the length, width, and height of each bag until I find one that fits the airline's maximum baggage allowance. I measure the bike frame and a new possibility emerges. If I completely disassemble the bike, removing the wheels and separating the frame into two pieces, it might be possible to fit the parts into three large bags. Excitedly, I order the bags and immediately get to work dissembling the bike. With renewed intentions, I return my focus to the island vision. Taking a calculated risk, I disassemble the entire bike into its component parts. I gamble, risking the entire trip on a hope and a prayer. My hope is that the parts will fit into several standard-sized checked bags. My prayer is that somehow, I'll find a way to reassemble everything on the other end.

The odds aren't in my favor; I've never taken apart or reassembled a bike like this before. Where I'm going there isn't a shop that'll be able to service the custom-designed mountain trike. A thousand things can't go wrong for the plan to work. A lost bag, a bent part, even a missing screw wouldn't be replaceable once I arrive at the big island.

Pulling out a GoPro camera, I film a time-lapse video disassembling the bike. I figure it might make a cute addition to the short film I'm planning to make, documenting my adventure. Balled-up newspaper and foam cushion the bike parts as I carefully pack them into three large bags. Thankfully, the parts all fit!

The next day, I stand proudly before the check-in counter with the three bags weighing just under fifty pounds each. I'd successfully disassembled the entire bike. Three stuffed bags would accompany me on the trip across the Pacific Ocean in airline-approved luggage. I'd worked through the first seemingly impossible limit of the trip.

The experience I gained from effectively navigating the airline baggage restriction provides unique insight into the nature of possibility. When dealt an impossible situation , I look to the limiting circumstance for an adaptation to find a way through instead of over it. I'm reminded that when we try to overcome the physical limitations imposed by the natural world by sheer force of will, we don't allow for new possibilities—we're living in denial of the truth. Awareness of my limits is where the possibility exists to move through them. I have a profound awareness that Parkinson's disease isn't a limitation to overcome; it's an invitation to live a life of possibility.

I must first acknowledge that there are certain physical limitations that do exist in reality. They're not to be overcome; they're to inform us of new possibilities and new actions to take. A *World Without Limit* exists like Zeno's paradox: within the very boundaries of physical existence is contained a space of infinite possibility. Paradoxically, infinite possibilities occur within a set of finite boundaries. Distinguishing limits is the first step towards determining a new opportunity-set of infinite possibility.

I feel empowered and a deeply gratifying sense of accomplishment. An elevated awareness of immutable physical limitations provides access to unlimited possibilities. I begin to associate with a new identity. I'm aware of the truth: Starting with an honest assessment of my limitations I begin to distinguish the way the world is, instead of the way I think it should be.

I'm on a path of possibility leading to discovery of a *World Without Limit.*

Chapter 12:

Paths of Possibility

The fears we don't face become our limits.

— *Robin Sharma*

July 2017: Kona, Hawaii

The plane barrels down the runway. Ascending through clouds, I gaze out the small oval window. Drifting in thought, I'm reminded of the heroic journey of Matthias Lanzinger, one of many who've inspired me to undertake this journey. His story exemplifies the life of a person who has discovered a *World Without Limit*. This begins with a willingness to acknowledge our natural limitations; and requires humility, not efforts of herculean proportion.

Matthias is disabled. The world-class Austrian skier crashed during a World Cup Super G run in 2008. Tumbling down the steep slope, he sustained a high-energy trauma resulting in an open-fractured leg break. His leg was amputated, leaving him with a natural limitation that ended any hope for Olympic ambitions.

Initially, resignation set in as Matthias acknowledged the injury that ended his skiing career. Facing grievous loss, he began to confront the fear that he'd no longer be able to compete at the Olympic level. Then something shifted in his perspective. He brought awareness to his limitations and began to focus on what he stood for—the possibility of returning to Olympic competition.

Mathias distinguished his limitations from his circumstances. He faced his fear, acknowledging the impact of a loss-of-limb injury. Simply having a desire to overcome impossible circumstances doesn't make the impossible, possible. To know truth is to see the world as it is, not as we think it is, or think it should be. Distinguishing circumstances for what they actually are is where the path to true freedom begins.

By bringing awareness to his limitations, Mathias was led to a new possibility: a prosthetic leg, and a dream to return to competition. Moving through the painful work of rehabilitation, he trained for the 2014 Winter Paralympics in Sochi. He went on to win two silver medals and that was just the beginning. Over the coming years he would win five more at the Alpine Skiing World Championships. An awareness of his natural limits and a commitment to fulfill his vision was enough for Matthias to obtain his goals.

The difference between Matthias and others in similar predicaments is his willingness to objectively distinguish natural limits from his vision of what's possible—he gets real about what he can and can't physically do. In doing so, he can discover adaptations within the boundaries of his limits that enable him to produce the results he intended and ultimately fulfill the possibility he created.

Matthias proves Zeno's paradox: within the boundary of limits is where the possibility of unlimited possibility exists. When limits remain undistinguished, no possibility exists. I learn an important lesson from Matthias: possibilities don't come to us, they arise from distinguishing the limitations within us.

While the differences between our physical disabilities are distinct, we share much in common. Loss-of-limb and loss of dopamine-producing neurons impose natural limits resulting from a physical disability. Today, there isn't a permanent cure for either of our conditions. Telling myself that I'll simply overcome Parkinson's is akin to Matthias telling himself he'll simply grow a new leg. Instead of resisting limitations, I choose to distinguish them, work through them, and take actions towards fulfilling my vision of a daring journey to the top of a volcano.

Along the way, Matthias and I were led to the adaptations necessary to achieving our dreams of accomplishment. Matthias was led to a prosthetic leg that enabled him to return to Olympic competition.

I was led to a pair of biomechanical brain implants with the possibility of riding a bike to the top of a volcano.

As I come to terms with the realities of my illness, I stop searching for possibilities beyond my limits and instead distinguish the limits' boundaries. New paths of possibility emerge. A spark ignites the spirit of hope, and inspiration is born. I experience a new vision; I'm a storyteller. I tell stories of possibility. In the vision, I see how these stories touch, move, and inspire countless others to see possibility from the confines of their own limitations. I confidently step into an unknown future, no longer filled with doubt and uncertainty. I know an alternative path will emerge.

***

The plane lands, and the journey begins. My friend, Taran, has traveled with me to help transport the Blue Rover and camera gear. We arrive at the Bay Club Waikoloa Resort condominiums at 3:00 p.m. I heft each of the weighty bags, one at a time, up two flights of stairs. A rattling mass of bike parts and camera mounts spill out onto the floor of the condominium's common area.

I momentarily stare in awe at the pile of parts, taking in the accomplishment of getting the bike to the island destination. Then reality sets in as I realize I have no idea how to reassemble the mass of bike parts back into their original state. I'd meticulously planned out my route. This means that in less than twenty-four hours, I should be on day one of the ascent up the volcano.

This isn't going to happen, I sigh, resigned to my circumstances.

A rush of optimism returns. *I've got this!* I say to myself.

I go to work, one piece at a time. Thankfully, I have the time-lapse video. I painstakingly proceed to watch it in reverse, retracing my steps.

Six hours later, the bike remains largely unassembled.

"I've bitten off more than I can chew," I say to the GoPro camera for the first day's video log. Having been awake the last thirty hours, I'm exhausted! *There's no way I'm going to be on my scheduled 10:00 a.m. ride tomorrow.*

"I'll get some sleep and see what it all looks like in the morning," I mutter, bleary-eyed, into the camera before crashing into a pile of the pillows on the soft resort bed.

At this point, I'll be lucky to be turning the cranks at all on this trip. Bummer, are my last thoughts as I drift off to sleep.

Floating through puffy clouds of a lofty delta-wave dream state, I'm drifting through eternity. Sleep spindles spiral softly as my mind consolidates subconscious memories of the previous night. Descending through peaceful theta waves, I make the final approach to consciousness. A soft landing through alpha waves is greeted by a subtle rise to a wakeful beta state.

My head rests comfortably, cushioned by a soft faux-goose-feather down pillow. Awakening to full consciousness, I'm in a pleasant, climate-controlled room. The thermostat holds a constant seventy-two degrees, maintaining the environment in a near-clinical state. Shielded from the muggy tropical island morning outside, I rest in a completely blissful state.

The unfamiliar room is heavenly. For the moment, a light brain fog clouds awareness of sore, jet-lagged limbs lying heavily in gravity-induced protest. As I attempt to rise from the opulent comfort of pressed Egyptian-cotton sheets, the battle begins.

When the natural limitations of Parkinson's had sufficiently progressed, doctors told me that I'd lost over eighty percent of my dopamine-producing neurons. This dopamine-hit resulted in both physical and mental resistances. The resulting combination has been a lethal one-two punch, severely depleting motivation: a multi-headed hydra I've battled daily.

I awaken, and the war to motivate is on. Muscle tightness grapples with mental lethargy. I force myself into the learned routine of what movement disorder specialists call a bed transfer. Rising to a seated position in a deliberate motion, I rotate my hips parallel to the mattress, firmly planting my feet into a balanced stance. My arms extend outwards as I lean forward into gravity. My quadriceps engage as I push off from my heels into a leg-press motion, lifting my 180-pound frame. Transfer complete! I wobble off towards the well-appointed hotel bathroom.

A spa-like shower rains down, massaging sore muscles. Tight shoulders soften as warm jets of water pulsate from a pair of shower-heads built into the wall. My stiff body relaxes as tensions ease. Puffy wisps of cloudlike steam rise into bright halogen lights hanging over the vanity mirrors.

Dripping, I step into the warm, moist, foggy room. I grab a velvety white oversized towel folded neatly on a bamboo shelf and plunge my face into it. I exhale a muffled breath into the soft texture, taking in its freshly laundered scent. I wipe away the condensation from the mirror, and for a foggy moment, I don't recognize the face looking back at me.

Who am I? I wonder.

I'm not prepared for what happens next. Greeted by a mass of bike parts strewn across the living area floor, a sense of dread creeps over me. I didn't know that I didn't know how to reassemble the rear derailleur, let alone how to engage the cassette. Cable-stay mounts lay across the floor like a giant game of pick-up sticks, presenting a confounding multidimensional puzzle.

Where do I even start?

"Coffee?" offers Taran, my travel companion and copilot for the expedition.

Kona coffee is arguably the best coffee in the world. I find no dispute as I take in the mocha aroma. Contemplating the dilemma represented by the mass of bike parts, I recall the recent experience at the airline counter.

Confronted by doubt, I bring awareness to the physical limitation I'm faced with. The solution resides in sitting with the discomfort of it. I don't have the knowledge or experience required to reassemble the bike. Sitting in the discomfort is painful. My mind wars, blaming myself, and the voice in my head rages.

I knew I shouldn't have taken this thing apart. There had to have been a better way to do this!

I open my laptop and begin surfing YouTube for the answer. Thousands of return searches clutter the screen with endless instructional videos on repairing derailleurs. It's not helping. The derailleur is uniquely configured for the recumbent design of the trike.

There's no solution to this problem! yells a belligerent internal voice.

I return to the discomfort of my circumstances and sit with the voice some more. There aren't any problems, just situations to be dealt with. Problems are just a point of view—a defiant voice that contributes nothing to resolve circumstances. I choose to focus on the solution instead of the problem, knowing an answer will emerge.

***

I still can't reassemble the bike.

In silent discomfort, the blaming voice takes on a more empathic tone. *This is a challenging circumstance—one that's not readily overcome. It's okay to be uncomfortable. Discomfort's necessary for comfort to return. Move through it.*

Cloudy thoughts begin to clear, and an empty sky-blue void emerges. In the growing space of nothingness, I recognize there isn't room for moral judgement. The voice that critiques my circumstances is crowded out by an expanding, empty space. There aren't any problems to solve, and there's nowhere to go, nothing to do; there's only the discomfort of sitting in an uncomfortable situation.

On the other side of nothing is everything, and inside of everything, anything is possible.

I breathe deeply into the uncomfortable space, and my body relaxes. The nirvanic state of nothingness is interrupted with a new thought. *Action!* My bike isn't building itself. I take the next step. *Starting from nothing, there's only right now, and the next step to take.*

I open my laptop, rerunning the time-lapse footage backwards again. Frame-by-frame, piece-by-piece, moment-by-moment, I'm present to the next action I need to take to rebuild the bike. I'm in action, moving through all the fear and discomfort that'd been there moments before, preventing action.

In what seems like the next moment, I stand before a completed bike that works! The crankshaft turns, the gears engage, and the bike functions as designed.

Who am I? I'm something from nothing, possibility and choice. A new reality materializes into physical existence as I continue to take the next action.

Chapter 13:

Elevate Awareness

Each is given a list of rules;

a shapeless mass; a bag of tools.

And each must fashion, ere life is flown,

a stumbling block, or a stepping-stone.

— Robert Lee Sharpe

July 2017: Waikoloa Hawaii, Day One, Ascent

I heave the massive Blue Rover over a red-and-white, candy-cane-striped gate near the Queens Highway on the west side of the Big Island. Ancient petroglyphs mark the entrance to an unnamed trailhead. Encumbered by custom camera mounts and a drone strapped to its belly, the Blue Rover adds nearly sixty pounds to my body mass.

Taran and I pick our way through a rocky lava path towards our intended starting point at the shoreline. Brakes squeal as I slow the descent of the Blue Rover to match her walking pace. Leaving the Queen's Highway behind, we make our way to an unnamed location, somewhere between the map-marker labeled "Lone Palm" and the "Lava-Lava Beach club."

Rumbling down the uneven trail we emerge onto a secluded white sand grotto. The Blue Rover finds a peaceful resting spot, cooling off in the clear Pacific water.

I've made it.

Exhaling a deep sigh of relief, a feeling of accomplishment washes over me. Removing the hard, stiff bike cleats and overheated compression socks, bare feet sink into soft sand. Standing next to the Blue Rover, I wiggle my toes in the cool water. Peering out into the horizon, crystal waves lap against the sturdy frame in a rhythmic antiphon.

I'm in paradise.

Reaching for the GoPro, I capture some footage of the Blue Rover's rear tire in the ocean. It's the dream I'd long envisioned in my mind's eye; it's exactly as I'd imagined it. It's as though I've been here before. It's the feeling of being in eternity, unbound by time.

Whup, whup, whup. The drone's blades cut through salty air as I nervously navigate it over crashing Pacific Ocean waves that pound against a black lava-rock shoreline. I feel a rush of adrenaline. One false move, a strong gust of wind, or a sharply cresting wave might send the drone plummeting into the ocean. I cautiously return the drone safely back to the shore, having successfully captured stunning aerial views of the Blue Rover resting in clear blue water.

Mounting the Blue Rover, we set out on our journey. Taran dutifully marches behind me as we ascend the warpath. Our conquest to summit the volcano has officially begun. Brimming with optimism, with the victory of rebuilding the bike still fresh in my mind, I forge confidently ahead.

I've got this!

Prior to the trip, I'd meticulously planned each day's route using the mileage and elevation details provided by Google Earth. There aren't any official trails that provide ready access to Mauna Kea from the west side of the island. The route I intend to traverse doesn't appear on any trail map. I'd stitched together a series of access roads, hiking paths, and stretches of unused highways to complete the ascent over a four-day period. The makeshift map I've created is printed on a series of eight-and-a-half-by-eleven laminated sheets of office paper.

Our initial plan had been to rebuild the Blue Rover immediately upon arrival. With the bike reassembled, I'd intended to run through a brief trial to work out any kinks. The short, one-mile trek from the shoreline to the Queen's Highway would serve as a warm-up in preparation for our weeklong journey.

Unfortunately, the fiasco reassembling the bike hadn't gone as planned. I'm now running a day behind schedule. This was understandable, given the mass of parts lying on the hotel floor less than

twenty-four hours ago. I allow myself some grace for the miscalcula-
tion, knowing it'd mean I'd have to work a little harder to catch up,
adding the warm-up segment to the first-day's ride.

The makeshift Google Map illustrates an initial approach, taking
us along a relatively easy, minimal-gradient path cut directly through
lava rock. The mile-long segment gradually rises to an elevation of
150 feet. While the distance and elevation statistics are well within
reach, the warm-up holds unanticipated surprises.

Instead of the compacted gravel roads I'd grown accustomed to
training on in Colorado, the volcanic trail is comprised of pulverized
lava. Known by native Hawaiians as *a'a*, this type of lava rock is
characterized by an extremely rough and sharp texture formed by
violent eruptions. Erosion and countless footsteps have flattened the
sharp-textured rock. The now-smoothed texture feels more like river
stones than lava rock, and it sinks several feet deep in places. The
loose stone causes the rear wheel of the Blue Rover to spin uncontrollably. It's nearly impossible to gain traction.

The planned warm-up turns into a grueling two-hour trial of
uneven fits and starts. The pedals randomly slip through large pools
of small loose stone.

"Uggghhh," groans Taran as she helps me force the Blue Rover
past several impassable sections of the trail. At several tight spots I'm
forced to dismount and pick up the bike to coax it through. *This isn't
going well.*

Panting hard, we finally arrive back at the entrance to the Queen
Kaahumanu Highway.

"We're going to have to rethink our approach, Taran," I mutter
in frustration.

"I'm hungry. Let's get some lunch. I think we'll both feel better
after we've both had a chance to rest," she cheerily replies.

"Yeah, maybe you're right," I say, hopeful that conditions for the
second leg of the trip will improve.

My spirits drop. *We're not going to make it.*

July 2017: Waikoloa Hawaii, Day Two, Ascent

After a night recovering in the hotel, I'm back at it. "Let's shift the approach and ascend the volcano from the shoulder of a nearby highway," I say, rubbing my sore legs from the previous day's excursion.

"Okay, I'll drive ahead of you, like a pace car," offers Taran.

I'm relieved. The highway is littered with makeshift grave markers, memorializing what happens to adventurous bikers who've braved the highway shoulders. "Share the road" is the mantra of road bikers the world over. The markers are evidence of how ineffective that mantra is.

Cars whiz by as Taran navigates the transport van along Waikoloa Road. Disregarding the speed limit, traffic regularly passes at speeds exceeding seventy miles per hour. I'm grateful for Taran's patience. Hazard lights flashing, the pace car meanders slowly along the shoulder behind me, sheltering the Blue Rover from excessively speeding traffic.

Turning the pedals rhythmically along the smooth pavement of the highway shoulder, traction is no longer an issue. The planned five-mile stretch rises over a thousand feet, connecting the shoreline resort complex with Waikoloa Village. The re-approach seems to be a perfect solution to make up for the previous day's missed milestone.

I'm getting back on track!

Pedaling the Blue Rover's stiff cranks, I push hard into the constant pull of gravity. I struggle to climb, carrying a total mass of nearly 250 pounds against me. With high hopes, I plunge headstrong into day two's ascent on Mauna Kea.

I'm met with an immediate headwind. Huffing and puffing up the mountain, I'm breathing hard.

The Blue Rover's computer barks, "Distance, one mile. Heart rate, 135 bpm. Cadence, 82 rpm." All within my expected parameters.

"Elapsed time, thirty-one minutes, twenty-four seconds. Average speed, 1.9 miles per hour."

Under two miles per hour? I'd averaged nearly four miles per hour in Colorado, and that was at fourteen thousand feet on a rocky, boulder-ridden trail with twice the grade. This should be easy compared to Cordova pass. *What's going on?*

Headwinds gust over thirty miles per hour. I'd planned on completing this leg in under two hours. Together with the steep grade of the highway, the five-mile leg of trip is taking nearly three times as long as planned.

Dealt with another physical limit beyond my control, I'd not anticipated thirty-mile-per-hour headwinds. Deep disappointment sets in. Determined, I double my efforts.

"Distance, two miles. Heart rate, 142 bpm. Cadence, 87 rpm. Elapsed time, forty-eight minutes, fifteen seconds. Average speed, 1.4 miles per hour," the Rover tells me.

My stats are getting worse!

I pause after two hours of grueling exertion. Legs burning, I walk over to the transport van to consult with Taran.

"What do you think?" I ask, trying to mask my disappointment.

"Looks like you're pretty tired. I don't think we're going to make the planned ascent today."

The reality of missing my goal feels terrible. I'd gotten this far, and to miss my second day's milestone is demoralizing.

"We've got to get out of this wind. Let's get to a higher elevation and find a trail somewhere off the highway," I offer skeptically, hoping to salvage some of the day's effort.

"Okay, but how are we going to make up the distance and elevation we've missed out on for the past two days?"

"Like you said, it's not going to happen," I utter in resignation.

I load the bike into the van and we venture out looking for an access point to continue the ascent from a higher elevation. Rising through several microclimates, we travel through beautiful, mostly barren landscapes. I'm aware of the Presence in the ancient land-mass. Something stirs deep within the volcano. The island's alive, growing. Only 300,000 years old, Hawaii is the largest and youngest of the island chain. Oahu, less than two hundred miles away, is three million years old.

What's that?" I spy a dirt road off to the left side of the main roadway. "Looks like an access road."

The transport van grinds up a short gravel path to a small wooden hut about a hundred yards alongside the off-road trail. A sign hanging above the small empty structure reads: "Kilohana Hunter Checking Station."

I get out of the transport van and step onto a rocky gravel road. It feels strangely familiar. "Hey, this stuff feels like what I trained on in Colorado!" I say. "I think I'll be able to get some good traction here."

Twenty minutes later, I'm pushing hard into the pedals, climbing steadily. "Distance, one mile. Heart rate, 142 bpm. Cadence, 91 rpm. Elapsed time, twenty-two minutes, forty-six seconds. Average speed, two-point-six miles per hour," the Rover tells me. While I know I'm not tracking remotely close to the path I'd planned for the second day of the trip, at least I'm making significantly more headway than I'd been when fighting thirty-mile-per-hour headwinds.

At just under the two-hour mark, I pause. I'm exhausted, and I've barely made fifteen hundred feet of elevation gain over a four-mile trek. The original day-two plan had us ascending over four thousand feet along a nineteen-mile ride. I'd trained for months to ensure this goal would be well within the limits of my reach. Reality sets in as the limitations of time and energy present themselves. My planned ascent for the day is unquestionably out of reach. For a second day, I'm overwhelmed by the physical limitations of my circumstances. My spirits sink yet again as I rise from the bike, both mentally and physically exhausted.

Standing alone in the silence, I contemplate my predicament. I've traversed four miles up the off-road trail, and there's nothing in sight other than the vast horizon before me. I'm completely alone, and there's nothing surrounding me for two-thousand-miles in any direction.

Something peculiar arises in the silent nothingness of the moment. A familiar sensation, the Presence, is with me in the silence. Closing my eyes, I take in a deep breath. *I'm alive.* More than just conscious of this moment, *I'm aware.* Like an ancient remembering, the sensation transports me back to the darkness where I'd first experienced the Presence before becoming conscious of IT. I find myself beyond the dark void in a place where time doesn't exist. Present to this moment, I'm given a gift rarely experienced: an acceptance and full understanding of myself as a being both unique and part of a universal experience—what I am, what I am not, what I can be. Heidegger famously refers to this place as "the clearing":

> *In the midst of beings as a whole an open place occurs. There is a clearing, a lighting . . . Only this clearing grants and guarantees to us humans a passage to those beings that we ourselves are not, and access to the being that we ourselves are."*
>
> *—Martin Heidegger*

I return to the passage of time. Thousands of miles away from any major landmass, I experience a growing awareness of the Presence in the dark. With each passing second, I sense the island growing, breathing. Mother Earth is alive. I stand at the threshold between land and sky. Magma rises from unknown depths far below the surface. I feel the earth breathing in life before each exhale, creating an expansion beneath my feet.

Volcanic eruptions generate more than an acre of new land to the island every week. This is equivalent to a fourteen-inch circle of land every second. I peer down at my feet and realize that I'm standing on exactly a fourteen-inch circle of volcanic soil. *It's alive!*

I'm profoundly struck by the physical connection I share with the earth. As I breathe, I'm connected to a oneness, a singular threshold between the sky above and the expanding landmass below. There is no separation.

There are no limits in this place, no obstacles to overcome. There aren't objectives, milestones, or goals to be attained; there are no expectations for performance or results. When I came to the island, I'd expected to complete a fourteen-thousand-foot continuous ascent from shoreline-to-summit. What I've instead discovered is an elevated sense of awareness for what matters most: compassion, empathy, and connection. Love and gratitude for myself and others. Care for our planet, the animals, plants, and trees. An awareness of the timeless rocky landscape, more ancient than life itself. A *World Without Limit*, free of expectation, with an access to living life fully in each passing moment. In this moment, everything in the universe is whole, perfect, and complete.

July 2017: Waikoloa Hawaii, Day Three, Ascent

The Blue Rover rattles restlessly in the back of the transport van as we ramble past the Kilohana Hunter Station. Our plan is to traverse across Lava Road, a narrow-paved stretch of unused highway cut into the high desert rock of the Humu'ula Saddle. Serving as the only access to this inhospitable landscape, Lava Road was once part of Old Saddle Road, formerly considered the most dangerous highway in the state. The otherworldly terrain is unlike anywhere else on the planet. True to its namesake, the road passes through lava flows resulting from the eruptions of 1984. Dark-gray magma extends in every direction in a moonscape of impassible, razor-sharp *a'a* lava rock.

I'm struck by an eerie, lifeless sensation. The Presence is here, though it's not welcoming to life as we know it. It's more ancient, existing before the vegetation and creatures came to occupy this place. I'm aware that the Presence was here long before the beginning, and that it will be here long after we've left.

Two and a half miles into my trek, I pull over to capture the emptiness of this place on video. Against all odds, standing twenty yards away is a lone *ohi'a lehua* tree. Protruding from somewhere deep within the steely volcanic surface, it has somehow managed to find a way to grow in this uninhabitable lava field.

Amazingly, the tree is flowering! Vibrant, bright-red pods sprout from dry limbs, creating a stunning contrast against the bleak dark-gray landscape. Picking my way through chunks of huge sharp stones, I creep along towards the mystical tree to get a closer look. Grinding sounds of cinderblocks scraping together accompanies each uncertain step. Spying a long flat stone that appears stable, I take a long stride forward. The unsteady rock lurches with the sound of an immense boulder rolling back from an ancient tomb. Rocking back and forth, my arms flail as I desperately try to find balance. I blindly reach out, pressing my palm into a large piece of nearby rock. My hand burns as a scalpel-like razor edge penetrates with surgical precision. Thankfully, I receive only a paper cut. Licking my wound, a metallic taste serves as a cautionary reminder.

Obscured by a mass of dark-gray lava rock, the undernourished tree emerges from the bone-dry high mountain desert. I'm struck by the powerful example of the spirit of nature. Rising from desolate terrain, this lone *ohi'a lehua* has managed to adapt itself to grow in the moon-like environment.

Pausing to rest in the vast field of barren lava rock, I'm present to the natural limits imposed on the beautiful flowering tree. Indigenous only to Hawaii, the *ohi'a lehua* grows over one hundred feet under ideal conditions. The natural environment of the high desert lava field has limited this specimen's growth to a mere ten feet.

Observing the tree, I'm aware that it doesn't fight against nature. Instead of resisting, it naturally finds the limits of its environment and adapts. There's an instinctual awareness of its natural limitations and an unseen power that pulls for its life. Unlike human beings, the tree doesn't endlessly complain and protest, *I'm not getting enough water, it's too hot here.* The tree doesn't question, *Why was I made to take root in the middle of this lava field?* The tree doesn't compare itself to those growing in the rainforest, wondering, *Why did I only grow to be ten feet tall? All the other trees have grown to over a hundred!*

Since arriving at the island, I've fallen short of every milestone I've set. I've questioned the progress I've made. I've doubted the results I've achieved. Over a year ago, sitting in a bike shop in Austin, I'd conceived the idea to ride to the top of Mauna Kea. I raised money from friends and family to help with expenses. I trained tirelessly for months, traveling to Colorado for high-altitude endurance training. I attended film school to produce a documentary of the expedition. I hired an editor and publisher to help produce this book. And yet, the voice in my head protests, judging. I've not produced the results I intended. I've not achieved the milestones I'd set out to accomplish. I've fallen far behind on my daily elevation and mileage targets. It's become painfully clear that the ascent won't be completed as planned. Doubt, resignation, and cynicism—the natural state of being human—sets in.

Against the barren backdrop stands this odd tree, its brilliant red flowers exploding with aliveness and beauty. It stands alone amidst this vast lava field. I'm deeply humbled. Being here in this moment, I'm aware of the futility of my doubts and fears.

The tree lacks water from its natural environment in the same way my brain lacks dopamine-producing neurons. Like the tree, I find myself living in a body lacking some critical elements of nature. I've been dealt an unplayable hand—one with real physical limitations.

What choices do I have? Do nothing? Accept my circumstances as they are? I'm left with a flat, numb feeling of inauthenticity. Acceptance doesn't honor my anger, my fear, my defiant spirit. Doing nothing is resistance, not acceptance.

For many years I've felt pulled between extremes of accepting my circumstances or resisting. Fighting a disease without a cure is exhausting. Like the *ohi'a lehua*, I realize there's a third path; instead of resisting or accepting, I'll adapt. *Acceptance without adaptation is resignation.*

Our culture thrives on stories of beating the odds, overcoming the impossible. "Fight, resist, overcome" echo in our defiant chants. These are the attitudes I've been encouraged to adopt when facing the giant of my impossible situation. It's exhausting, and unnecessary. I discover that resisting, fighting, trying to overcome the impossible all detract from living life fully in this moment.

Complacent resignation, or simply accepting my circumstances, is also not a way of being fully alive. There *is* a next action to take—a direction to move towards. It starts with an awareness of the natural limits of my physical environment. An awareness of physical limitations leading to adaptations enables a *World Without Limit* to emerge as possibility.

I return to the bike and pedal back to the transport van. I've achieved my objective without knowing what it was. Recognizing the limits that've brought me to this place, a new world unfolds before me: a *World Without Limit*. A world of unlimited possibility revealed by the natural physical limits of my environment. I acknowledge the futility of resisting. No longer burdened by overcoming the impossible, I wonder, *What's now possible?*

I'm reminded that who I am is the possibility of unlimited possibility.

We conclude the third day of the ascent and return to the hotel for much needed rest and recovery.

July 2017: Waikoloa Hawaii, Day Four, Ascent

The next morning, I watch the cheery weatherman on the local news. "Eighty percent chance of precipitation across much of the island today."

"Hey, Taran, this doesn't look good."

"What's up?" she asks, peering over steam rising from a generic white hotel coffee mug.

"Looks like the volcano's not going to cooperate today. Can you check out the weather report on your phone?"

"Uh-oh," she confirms between sips, cradling the warm mug in her hands. "You're right, looks like rain is forecasted all morning."

"Let's head up anyway," I reply. "You never know what the God of rain might not deliver, conditions change on the volcano hour-by-hour."

"Okay, but don't be disappointed if your last day's a blowout. Are you sure you don't want to just tour the island today? I'd love to get a picture at Rainbow Falls."

"And miss out on the final ascent of the trip? No way! I don't care if I have to climb up an erupting volcano on my hands and knees, I'm going for it!"

"All right, then you drive—I've no confidence on those steep mountain roads."

The van sputters and we embark into the uncertain, rainy morning. We race along Saddle Road as eighteen-wheelers kick up clouds of misty droplets that pelt the windshield.

"Doesn't look like this is gonna let up," Taran mutters disappointingly, and we make the turn up the access road. Speeding past the Mauna Kea visitor center, the sign reads,

"WARNING—Hazardous road, travel at your own risk beyond this point." The seven-mile stretch of the access road winds its way up the volcano and traverses along dozens of serpentine switchbacks. Small boulders litter the gravel road, creating a maze of obstacles as we begin the day's ascent. Peering into the rear-view mirror, I see a cloud of ash. Rumbling from behind is a sinister monster-of-a-sound. Something's quickly approaching. A huge plume of volcanic dust spews forth from beneath what appears to be a large caterpillar tractor.

I recall the park ranger's warning from the visitor center: "Watch out for the grazers."

Pulling off to the left side of the road, dangling keys rattle against the steering column as we watch the heavy equipment rumble by. A large grate dragged by thick chains pulverizes the boulders strewn about the road into more navigable terrain. The van winds its way up a death-defying twenty-two-percent grade as we continue the trek upwards. My body presses into the back of the seat as the gravity of our situation unfolds. The summit remains high above, somewhere through the ominous gray clouds.

"This is insane, I can't believe how steep this is!" Taran exclaims.

"Yeah, I've never been on a road quite like this before," I answer. "I grew up driving rocky mountain passes in Colorado, and normally I've got a pretty good constitution for this sort of thing, but man, this is frightening!" I'm scared. That familiar feeling of fear, indistinguishable from excitement, pulses with adrenaline. The sound of gravel, crushed under the weight of the transport van, gives way to silent smooth pavement and we cross over to the upper section of the Mauna Kea access road. Shortly after the road smoothens out, and we ascend through the dark clouds, passing through a threshold like an airplane that's just taken off. The foggy atmosphere gradually fades away and we emerge above the cloud line. The sun bursts onto the scene, shining magnificently against a canvas of deep blue sky.

"Wow, that's amazing! Five minutes ago, we were in the midst of foggy rain clouds, and now there's not a cloud in the sky!" exclaims Taran.

"Yes!" My heart leaps out of my chest, joyfully greeting the warm, brightly glowing sun. "I can't wait to get to the top, it's so beautiful!"

Climbing to the final reaches of the volcano summit, our spirits are lifted. Having made the symbolic transition over the cloud threshold into the bright, sunny-blue sky, I feel transformed.

"Okay, today's intention is to ride the final segment from the Umikoa Trail to the observatory towers," I announce, pulling into a parking space next to the Gemini Observatory. Opening the door, I'm greeted by stiff, chilling, biting winds. The peak of Mauna Kea is nearly fifty degrees cooler than the shoreline we'd left only a few hours earlier.

Taran stands dutifully beside me, preparing to film with the GoPro camera on a gimbal. Her shoulders squeeze together as she instinctually rocks to-and-fro, trying to warm herself.

"What do you think?" I ask.

"I think I'm going back in the van with the heater," she mutters skeptically through chattering teeth. "That drive up was intense. You sure you're up to riding this?"

I'm not convinced, but the observatories are calling to be filmed. "I'm just going to ride around up here a bit—get some good footage, then see how I feel."

"Okay, thank you—that sounds great. I'm not prepared to do the pace car thing, chasing you up the volcano. Besides, it's way too cold, you must be freezing!"

The excitement of reaching the summit is so overwhelming that I hardly notice the biting cold air. Unloading the Blue Rover from the transport, I attach three GoPros to the custom mounts I'd designed to capture footage from every direction. My stiff legs protest loudly; the end of the weeklong trek has taken its toll. I plop myself into the bucket seat and head out to the eastern volcano edge. The views are stunning. I'm literally and figuratively blown away. Peering over the guardrail, the side of the volcano drops off precipitously.

Making my way back over to the western volcano edge, I'm feeling light-headed. Gasping at the oxygen-depleted environment, my brain struggles to adapt to the thin air. Containing forty percent less oxygen than sea level, there's no wonder why my head's in the clouds! I'm grateful for the time I'd invested, training at altitude to prepare. The panoramic perspective from the summit is truly breathtaking. I'm on top of the world!

Panting, I gasp for air. Muscle tissue that has been torn and laced with lactic acid spasms in protest. Stretched too far by a tenacious mind, my body imposes definite limits. Diligent training and perseverance have pushed me to discover what those limits are. This has been my self-prescribed test; the reason thousands of miles were ridden—the reason why months of preparation and training were necessary.

Arriving at the top of the volcano, I stand at the summit. I pause to celebrate all that's transpired. I sit with feelings of judgement, both good and bad, associated with the experiences of living a life fully lived—my journey's taken me from unbounded misfortune: Parkinson's disease, divorce, and alcoholism, to the joy and victories of facing adversity and unlimited possibilities. I've amassed a small fortune and lost it all. I've had quite a story to tell—and it's just a story, probably not so different than your own in certain respects.

The truth is, what happened, happened. The rest is my endless evocation of a never-ending drama, conjured meanings that I choose to add to the happenings of life. *It is what it is,* and *it isn't what it isn't. I did what I did, and I didn't do what I didn't do.*

As the agent of choice, my entire life fits into the actions I take right now. I'm responsible for the choices I make and the actions I take. The rest is just the story I tell and I'm free to add any meaning I choose. I might add significance to it, or not. My life is a series of meaningless happenings made significant by a mind full of doubt and fear that attaches meaning to everything.

I have endless questions without answers and an uncanny ability to generate uncertainty.

I'm still filled with fear and doubt; strangely, I take comfort in the idea that I'm pretty sure you are too. Gazing into the face of fear, I feel it, and in the next moment I'm free to act and be who I choose. The face of fear isn't fearless, nor fearful. I'm not paralyzed by it, nor am I trying to overcome it. Simply being present to it is enough. There's nothing to do with it, other than to be with it, and that's how it's defeated.

In this moment I discover a new feeling: accomplishment. I am the Observer of accomplishment, the Watcher. I observe that accomplishment is actually a feeling, and I want more.

"More of what?" asks the Watcher.

"I can't be certain," IT responds.

I'm afraid. What if I don't get any more? What if I never find it?

"That would be good," replies the Watcher.

The questions of the mechanical mind are relentless and never-ending. I observe the machinery hard at work. Doubting, questioning, searching for the answer, IT grinds away. IT wants to be certain.

Epilogue

Eternity: In the Presence of the Here and Now

I emerge in the present moment. I'm here. Arriving from an infinitesimally minute slice of time between *now* and *what happens next*, I stand in Heidegger's "clearing," the place between past and future. I discover limits that've already been pre-determined. In the next moment, I discover that they're not really limits—only a point of view that can be transcended. I'm the author of my life, living fully into a future of my choosing.

My journey has taken me to the edge of my limits, to the place where the only way of being was being fearless. I no longer plunge toward a frightening, uncertain future. I am the possibility of unlimited possibility.

The Presence is here in the darkness—I sense it, I remember it. I recognize that it never left the dark void of the vast room before my story began; I'd only temporarily lost awareness of it.

Don't you sense its presence? I ask IT.

"Yes, and it's good," IT says.

What's good? I ask

"Good?" IT replies, rhetorically. "Good is the absence of *not-good*. The Presence in the darkness has returned to your awareness. Good is a choice."

Oh, I say confused. *I guess this existence isn't not-good.*

"Yes." IT concludes the conversation. "It is what it is."

Don't you mean I am what I am? I laugh.

There's only silence in response. The rumble monster remains; that old actor isn't going anywhere. For now, he lies lurking in the darkness. The response of "I'm Outta Here" awaits, prepared to leap into action at the first sight of deep emotions. I'm certain of that.

While writing this book, I've discovered the answer to the question, *who am I?* I'm the one who asks the question, and the one who questions the answer. Standing in the inquiry, a more meaningful question arises: *Who are we for each other?* These are my answers:

- *We are* perfect children of a loving God.

- *We are* possibility, our intentions, and the declaration of our word.

- *We are* what we're committed to, and the next action we take.

- *We are* transforming as we lift each other up, guided by our highest self.

Lastly, I've realized that I really don't want to know the answer to the question, "*who am I?*" I'm rediscovering who I am in each passing moment; now, isn't that an exciting adventure?

The answer to the question *who am I?* is contained in the question itself. *I am* the universe discovering itself, asking its most basic question, and continuously recreating the answer. *Who am I?* contains a more relevant question: *What's possible?*

What's possible? isn't a question. It's an opportunity to explore a life fully lived—a life of unlimited possibility. Paradoxically, a *World Without Limit* becomes possible when we gain an elevated awareness of our limitations. I invite you to come play! Let's write our next chapter, ascend to the summit of our mountaintop, and face our fears together. Let's rediscover what it means to return to ourselves as we descend into peaceful valleys. Life's an exciting adventure, unfolding within each of us. Our future is shaped only by the significance we choose to give to its passing.

There's no limit to our imagination. The paradox of unlimited possibility awaits our rediscovery, arising from within boundaries of a *World Without Limit.*

Acknowledgements

There have been many individuals and organizations who've traveled with me on this journey of self-discovery: teachers, healers, family, and friends whose loving support has made the writing of this book possible. Their collective contributions continue to guide me along new paths of possibility, inspiring hope. From challenges borne of adversity, they provide a space of grace where fear, doubt, and uncertainty are met with compassion, dignity, and gratitude.

Teachers

To all my teachers, thank you. Your guidance has led me to victories over seemingly unplayable hands dealt in the game of life.

To the Presence, the dealer in this game, thank you. You teach me compassion, empathy, and forgiveness. You're the divine spark and the source of creation and all inspiration. You teach me to have faith, to hope, and to love, and I long for my return home to you.

To the darkness, whose presence is more ancient than the light, thank you. You're the place of consciousness. You instruct me with desire, informing me to distinguish what the right action is. I'm grateful for your contribution of distinction.

To the philosophers of the ages, thank you. You're the lovers of wisdom. You illuminate truth, ever reminding me to see the world as it is, not as I think it should be. C. G. Jung, Epictetus, Descartes,

Hegel, Schopenhauer, Heidiger and Nietzsche, thank you. And thank you to the Austin Philosophy and Discussion Group—Leonard, Don, and all those who participate in the conversation of truth.

To Landmark Worldwide, providing freedom and power to be effective in the areas of life that matter most to me, thank you. Your instruction has taught me to live an extraordinary life and to redefine what's possible. Werner Erhard, Janet Zaretsky, Andrew Pole, Sarah Chappell, the Landmark community in Austin, and all those who participate in the worldwide community of transformative learning—thank you.

Healers

To all those who've helped me to heal, thank you. You've given me the gift of aliveness, enabling me to rise to the challenge of being the change in the world I hope to see.

To my doctors, clinicians, and care providers, thank you. Thank you to Dr. Robert Izor and the staff at Neurology Solutions Movement Disorders Center in Austin; Dr. Gordon Baltuch, Dr. Daniel Weintraub, and the staff at the Parkinson's Disease Movement Disorders Center in Philadelphia; Dr. Warren Olanow and the staff at the New York Neurological Institute at Columbia University; and the DBS team at Medtronic.

To my family's mental health professionals, counselors, therapists, and organizations that support recovery: thank you. You've given me the wisdom, strength, and hope needed to recover. You include: Kathleen Sheehan, the staff at Seton Mind Institute, Sky's the Limit Fund, Solstice East, Kyle Gillett, Bryan Tomes, Mark Dunn, the staff at Auldern Academy, Dr. Abraham Low, Recovery International, the recovery community in Austin, Yellow House Foundation, Hope Group, David R, Chris B, Timothy Q, Kurt R, Von L, Kenny Y, Joe Jeep, Jeff Lewis, Bill Wilson, and the fellowship of Alcoholics Anonymous.

To my spiritual guides and healers, thank you: Gerry Starnes, Nate "Owl" Long, and the Shamanic Community of Austin. And thank you to John O'Donohue, Bishop Robert Barron and the Catholic Church, Marty Shantz, and Patience Kim.

Family and Friends

To all those whom I lovingly call my friend, thank you. You've touched, moved, and inspired me to reach for what I thought was no longer possible, providing comfort and encouragement on our journey together.

To my daughter, Ashley, my light in the darkness, thank you. Your heroic journey of recovery and presence in my life are the greatest gifts I've ever received. May you always love yourself with the unconditional love that I have for you.

To my relatives, thank you: my mother and father, Linda and Leo Andron, my sister, Allison Trahan, Uncle Tom, Aunt Julie, Ian, and extended family; Eden Evans, Mimi Roth Paul, and Susan Evans.

To the partners and employees of Legacy Advisors, Clearbrook Financial, and all the clients who've been with me on this journey, thank you. You've given me the possibility of making a difference and have persevered through my struggles and challenges, always reminding me of what it means to be responsible: Jane Evans, Mike Pietrowicz, John Kroll, Vince Panvini, Richard Holt, John Morris, Christopher "Goose" Henderson, Fritz Beselaar, Brett Wayman, Charles Morton, and Walter and Terri Shikany. Thank you.

To those organizations and individuals who continue to provide support and encouragement for those with Parkinson's disease, thank you: Power for Parkinson's, Nina Mosier, Capital Area Parkinson's Society, MEYROW Foundation, Russell Meyerowitz, Davis Phinney Foundation, and the Michael J. Fox Foundation.

To those who continue to bless me with the gift of friendship, thank you: Karen Clark, Bob Sahm, Tom and Eleni Sowanick, Jason Sedmak, Scott Barbarick, Allan Hugh Cole Jr. Thank you.

To Taran Bhatia. Your partnership and contribution of time and energy made our journey to the top of Mauna Kea possible, and my lifetime dream a reality. Thank you.

Hero's

Lastly, to the hero's who battle Parkinson's Disease and other neurological impairments each day. Thank you for your living testimony, a revealing of the light of hope. You are the source of my gratitude, ever reminding me that life, in all its forms, is an unimaginable gift to be cherished. Contained within each of us is an adventure to unveil, a message to deliver, and a story to tell. Thank you.

About the Author

Alex Andron is an author, speaker, and former Wall Street broker. At age thirty-four, he was diagnosed with Young Onset Parkinson's Disease. After seven years of living with the challenges of a chronic, progressive movement disorder, he underwent a pioneering new surgery —a procedure that changed his life. *World Without Limit*, Alex's first publication, is the story of his life—his rise, fall, and recovery. Alex is a sixth-generation descendent of the Pfluger family from Pflugerville, Texas. He currently resides in Austin, near to his mother, father, and sister.